Images from Within

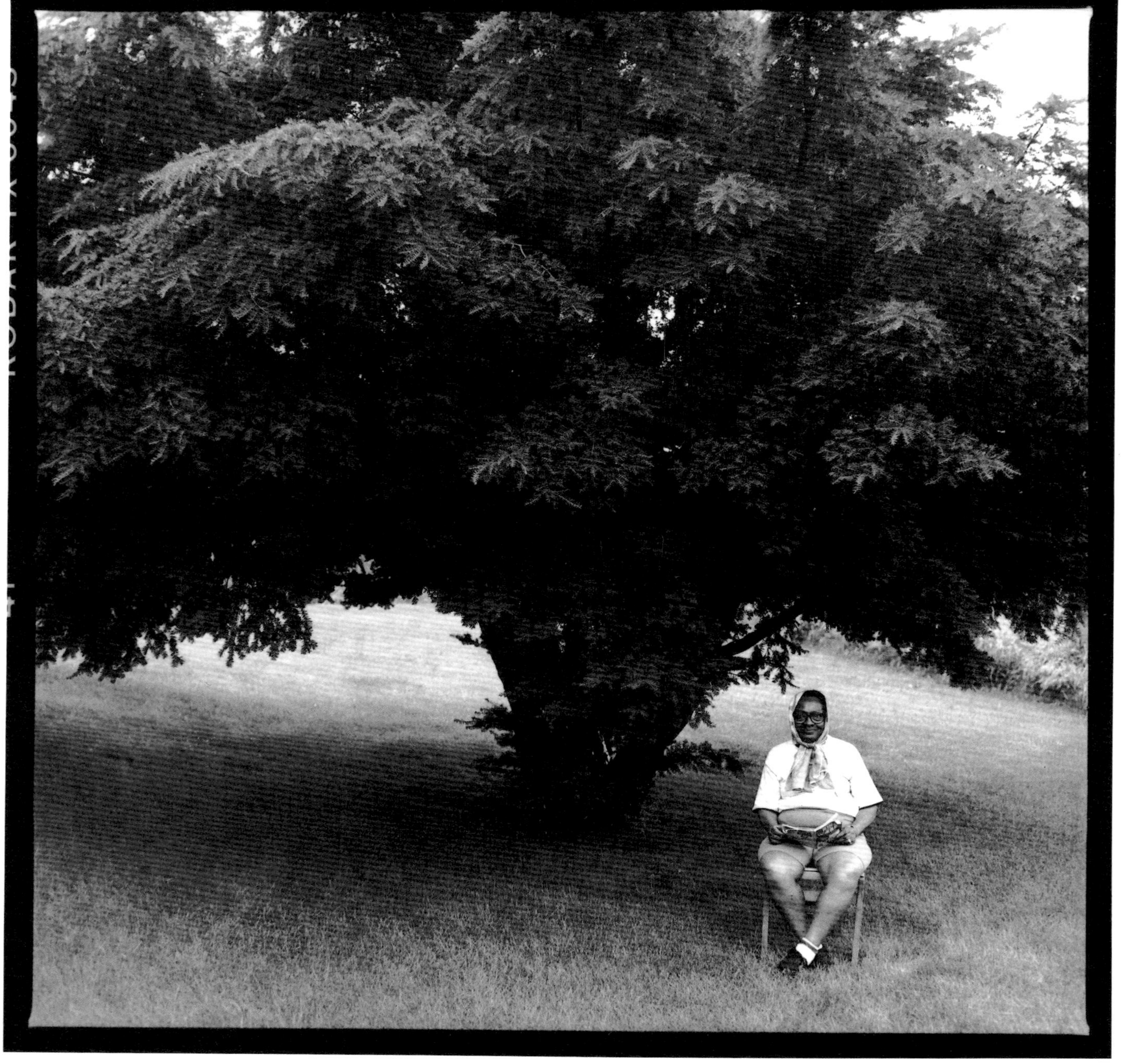

Images from Within

Portraits of People Confronting Mental Illness

Marc Hauser
images

Alisa Hauser
words

HIGH TIDE PRESS 1999

A HIGH TIDE BOOK

Published by High Tide Press Inc.

1910 Ridge Road, Homewood, Illinois 60430

toll-free / 888 487 7377

e-mail / hightideal@aol.com

Library of Congress Catalog Card Number: 98-74027

Hauser, Marc and Hauser, Alisa Images from within: Portraits of people confronting mental illness / by Marc Hauser & Alisa Hauser – 1st ed.

ISBN 1-892696-01-0

Printed in Hong Kong by C&C Offset Printing Co., Ltd.

04 03 02 01 00 99   6 5 4 3 2 1

Book design by Alex Lubertozzi

First Edition

Printed on acid-free paper. ∞

In memory of

Brian McGarry

Megan Tomasik

MaryLynn Wilson

Sidney Hauser

Come friends, the quick and the dead, from overseas and from the cemeteries. And if we have already managed to gather here so nicely, let's have a feast in the garden to beat all feasts.

— George Konrád

Lost in a dark, frightening forest;
I was alone with my fears
The forest felt like forever a trap;
I just barely knew that I needed help.

— Bruce Goodson

List of Illustrations

Acknowledgments

We would like to thank all of the staff members and friends of Trinity Services and the Lockport Center for Behavioral Health, Chris Stanley, Tim Tucker, and Britt Fohrman for making this project possible, and all the people receiving services at Lockport Center, whether photographed or not, for giving these pages a pulse.

A Special Thanks

To the Board of Directors of Trinity Services Inc.:

Art Dykstra

Barbara Hall

William Lipsey

William Long

S. Joseph Matesi

Raymond McShane

Al Olson

Tom O'Reilly

Anne Schauland

Kenneth Stromsland

And the Board of Trinity Foundation:

Robert Borgstrom

Deborah Gustafson

Herman Roche

Mike Sieling

George Troha

Foreword

> *"The present age is demented. It is possessed by a sense of dislocation, a loss of personal identity, an alternating sentimentality and rage which, in an individual patient, could be characterized as dementia."*
>
> — Walker Percy

Time was, when I was growing up, that people with mental illness were "put away" someplace so the rest of us "normal" folks didn't have to think about them. I now realize, as I look back with the benefit of age and experience, how distorted this was. To some extent, that was the way things were a generation ago.

Now, with greater knowledge and understanding, we recognize such separation and isolation is not wise or healthy, for the patients or the society as a whole. In this context it is interesting to note a recent study that reveals how Academy Award-winning films are reflecting a trend toward higher visibility for people with disabilities in our schools and society. In the article, "Lessons from Hollywood" (*Perspectives*, Spring-Summer 1998, Vol. II, No. I), Dwight Woodward writes, "In the period from 1927 to 1939 only one (2.6 percent) of the winners portrayed a person with a disability, while from 1990 to 1996 the number rose to nine (42.8 percent) of the total. Fifty-four percent of the films featured characters with psychiatric disturbance, by far the most common type of disability portrayed in the films studied … followed by physical disabilities, mental retardation, and autism."

Trinity Services provides an exciting and challenging alternative to this dilemma for the people who become a part of this community, the Lockport Center for Behavioral Health.

When Marc Hauser first talked with me about his work with "the Trinity Project," he said he was more excited about these photographs than any he had made in a long time. Once I saw the photographs, I understood his enthusiasm. This situation provides him with an opportunity to do what he does best — reveal in rich and eloquent visual images the physical likeness and, more profoundly, the soul and spirit of an individual. Marc is perhaps best known for his portraits of the rich and famous — Michael Jordan, Woody Allen, Aaron Copland, Sophia Loren, and countless others — and with good reason. But it is not simply that they are familiar faces, but that in his photographs he takes us beneath their façade. It is his ability to get a sense of the real person within that makes his pictures different from the typical celebrity shots we see in magazines and on posters. While the people in these photographs are not known to me, I do recognize their individuality and their humanity because of Marc's revealing eye and photographic skill.

In making these photographs, Marc is taking a risk. Away from the lights and controls of his studio, he has stripped the process to the essentials: Hauser, the small camera, perhaps a tripod, and the person. Thus the experience becomes a cooperative venture — not photographer and subject, but two individuals in collaboration with a camera between them.

As I examined these photographs, many memories came to mind and two stand out: the first was the parallel with Marc's earliest work, thirty years ago, when he was a high school student and yearbook photographer, and I was his photography teacher and yearbook faculty advisor. Then, too, he was documenting, with insight and sensitivity, a social and learning institution and producing visually strong and effective photographs. These images remind me of the consistent and revealing quality of his work, and how many exceptional pictures Marc has made in his career thus far.

The second memory is of more recent vintage. Several years ago I heard an interview with one of the men Richard Avedon photographed for his *In the American West* exhibition and book. The man, a drifter, had a grim history of depression, alcoholism, and attempted suicide. In the conversation he said, with tears rolling down his cheeks, that the Avedon portrait had literally changed his life. When he saw himself through Avedon's lens, in a life-size print in a major museum, he saw not what he was but what he could be. It is my hope and firm belief that such feelings will be evoked as the people in Marc's photographs discover themselves in these portraits.

In these photographs Marc has not only revealed and presented these remarkable people to us, but has reflected the individuals within back to themselves.

David G. Currie

Preface

The man moved a few steps back, studying his reflection in the bank window. He ran his finger lightly over his upper lip and smoothed back his black, wavy hair. From my rearview mirror, as I waited at the busy intersection, I continued to watch him watch himself. He seemed completely comfortable standing in front of the window in the same way that others stand before their bathroom mirrors. As I was turning, a young Hispanic woman walked up behind the man and surprised him. She tugged at his arm, and they both entered the bank building.

While driving away, I thought about the man I had just watched as well as other people I'd seen streaming in and out of the First National Bank of Lockport building. Some walked alone, while others walked in small clusters. A few wore sweaters despite the summer heat. Although they didn't appear to blend in with the lunchtime business crowd or the tourists perusing the antique shops, they seemed to belong on the quaint streets in the small, historic town. As a newspaper reporter, I was visiting Lockport to generate some future story ideas. At the bottom of my list was, "the bank building," followed by a question mark.

Upon returning to Lockport, I entered the "bank." Inside were many people sitting in the lobby or walking in and out of small rooms. The man I had watched was standing in a corner and talking quietly in Spanish with his girlfriend. Nearby, I overheard a man complaining to a woman about his roommate, who was drinking all the milk within hours of purchasing it from the store. "What should I do? It makes me mad!" he said. The woman, a counselor, urged him to talk calmly with his roommate and perhaps consider buying certain items separately.

There was so much activity in this building — phones ringing, a copier copying, numerous people having conversations. I talked with a secretary, and she directed me to Thane Dykstra. Moments later I met the young clinical director, who shares an office with a counselor in the bank's vault. In an effort to create the illusion of more space, they had creatively added a landscape poster of an alpine lake — the sort used by portrait studios — to one of the walls. Thane assured me that, yes, I was correct in noticing that the building was no longer a bank. He explained that all of the people in the building are living with a mental illness and attend therapy sessions and treatment groups throughout the day. He also told me about the Roxy, an old Lockport movie theater with a blank marquee about a block away, which is utilized as a recreational hang-out for the people served by the Lockport Center for Behavioral Health.

After scribbling a few pages of notes, I thanked Thane for taking time to chat with me. He seemed enthusiastic about the possibility of a newspaper story on the center and the people it serves. I eventually wrote the story, and five months later it still was not published. Girl football players, people who owned hand guns, and high school band camp were some of the stories that bumped the Lockport Center from the paper. It seemed strange to me that mental health treatment, which once captivated readers with its horrific scenes of institutional life as in *One Flew Over the Cuckoo's Nest*, was no longer interesting when it was humane and based in the community. Many of the people at Lockport Center had once spent time in sprawling, remote psychiatric hospitals, and today they were living in community houses or apartments and attending therapy groups in a downtown area. In my eyes, this was newsworthy. And yet the sentiment shared by others was to look away, not write any stories about it — especially for a new, community newspaper trying not to make too many waves.

But I didn't want to look away from people like Harold Leyerle, a former Air Force instructor and college graduate now working on treating his mental illness, or Sue Fencl, a mother and pool player with a sardonic nature, or Rose Clark, called "Ma" by her friends, who always has fresh baked goods to share. These people, as well as many others, had finally arrived at a place in which they felt secure enough to deal with their psychiatric diagnoses and work on changing their behavioral patterns. In addition, I did not want to ignore the warmth and friendliness the people of Lockport Center seemed to share as I observed them walking down the street or eating lunch in the windows of local sandwich shops.

This warmth and atmosphere of genuine caring eventually prompted another visit to Thane's office. This time I inquired about job openings. Soon after, with luck and a great deal of nervous energy, I was working with the people in their homes, assisting them with daily living skills, and helping with a creative writing group in the Roxy. I apologized to Rose Clark about the lack of a story, and she reluctantly told her relatives and friends who had reserved copies to stop waiting.

A few months later, I was grateful the story was never published, as it was written from the perspective of an outsider looking in. About the same time I discovered I had a distant cousin, Marc Hauser, a well-known portrait photographer. I did some research to find portraits of mentally ill people, but all I found were bleak images from the past — a lone person crouched in the corner of a cell, glassy-eyed women sitting around the recreation rooms of institutions in dirty gowns, close-up photographs of stitches on a frail wrist. The photographs were haunting, yet they spoke of a different era, when time was measured by staff shift changes and the blinking lights signifying medications. There were no photographs of people who had mental illness living and working in communities, leading positive lives with the support of a treatment program. I telephoned Marc and introduced myself as "a possible cousin," and explained my idea of photographing the people at Lockport Center in a different light, free of the darkness and obscurity one might expect to find in portraits of people with mental illness. He showed interest in the idea, and we sought and later received support from Art Dykstra and the board of Trinity Services, the non-profit, non-sectarian organization that launched the Lockport Center for Behavioral Health in 1991.

I began speaking directly with the people we serve about perceptions of mental illness and encouraged them to talk about the obstacles they have faced and overcome while living with mental illness. More than forty people responded to these questions. Some spoke of losing privileges to raise their children and drive a car. Others spoke of frustration over medications and the difficulty of keeping a job while suffering from depression. Nearly all of them spoke of attending therapy groups, working on managing and understanding their illness, and going back into the community to work. It became evident that they should write this book themselves, and I should act only as a recorder. My contribution was editing the interviews for space and to allow the portraits to speak for themselves. For those who wanted to be photographed, I asked them to select three or four places where they felt comfortable. Patsy Sims firmly wrote, "I want to be in the backyard of my house under the tree with the wind blowing." Coincidentally, that portrait is the cover of this book, and Patsy continued sitting beneath the tree long after Marc's shutter clicked for the last time that summer evening.

Patsy felt comfortable beneath her backyard tree in the same way that Arturo — the man standing in front of the bank window — seemed relaxed as he stared at his reflection. There are times in our lives when we want to escape the rhythm of our day — if only for a moment — and peer within ourselves asking, "What am I seeing, what are others seeing?" Photography is such a digression, and it has been a pleasure bringing the following people and fragments of their stories together.

Alisa Hauser

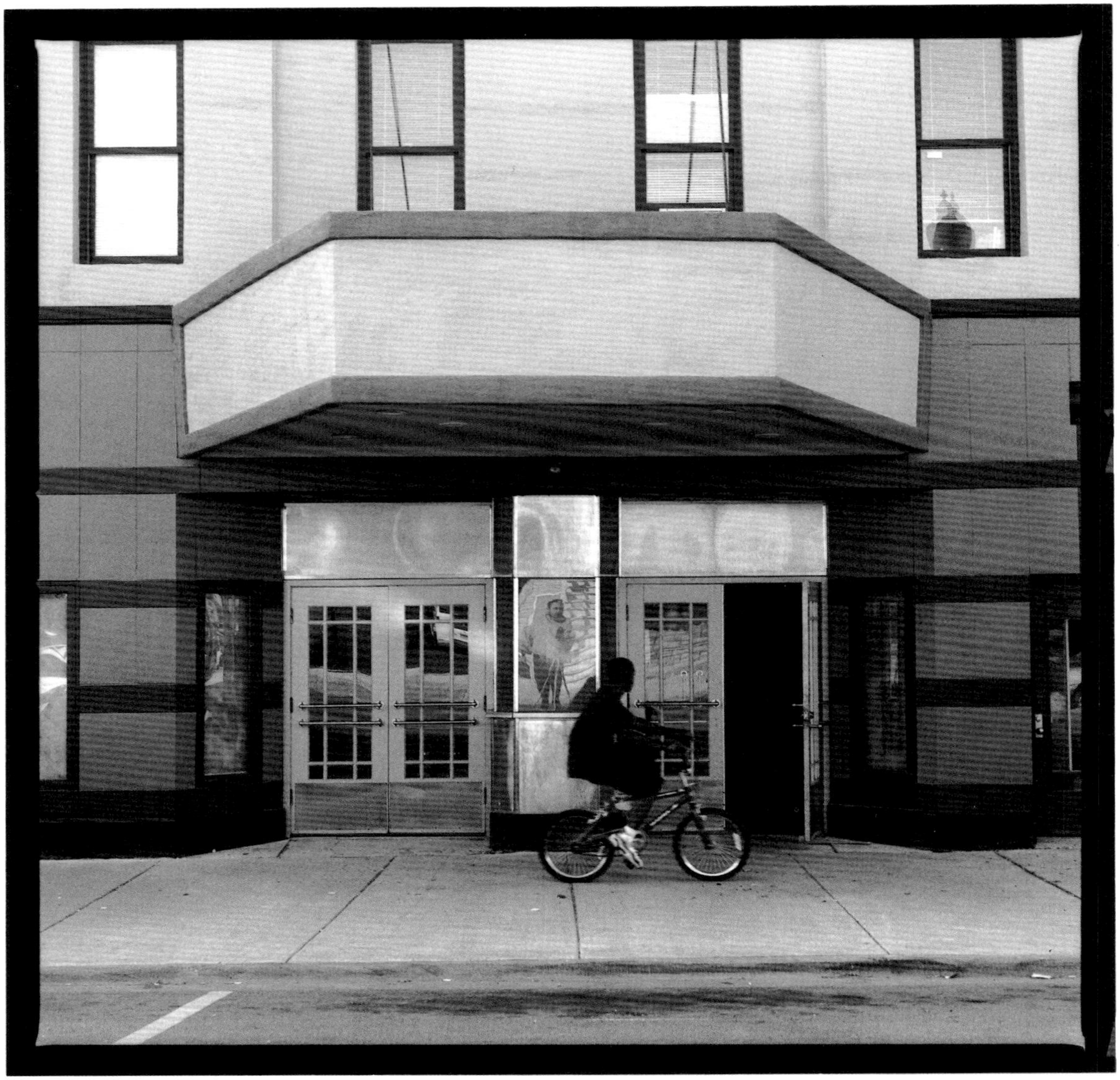

The Roxy Theater

Introduction — A Little History

Upon hearing that the Will County Health Department was planning to close its mental health treatment program, Art Dykstra, the executive director of Trinity Services and a long time advocate of the rights of people with disabilities, asked Sharon Parker to help draft a proposal for a mental health program at Trinity Services, an organization that had served adults with developmental disabilities since 1950. With nearly forty years of collective experience in the mental health field between them, they knew enough about what they didn't want to see in a program: hierarchy enhanced by too many offices, cruel mistreatment, and institutional living defined by excessive routine and uniformity. They knew they wanted to assist adults with mental illness in living independent lives, provide day and residential counseling, and offer affordable, community-integrated living arrangements.

Their proposal was successful, and their philosophies appealed to Mike Brown, Harold Hyde, and Tony Rivera. All three were facing the demise of their treatment program in 1991. With a $175,000 grant from Will County, the trio of Dykstra, Parker, and Bill Kahoun — an employee from Trinity who wanted to work in the new program — began hiring staff, opening a group home and beginning plans for a day treatment center. Thane Dykstra, Art's son who, as an infant, had accompanied his father to work at the Elgin State Mental Hospital and been passed around in the arms of patients, was completing his Ph.D. in clinical psychology at the University of Nevada-Reno. In 1995 he became the clinical director of the Lockport Center.

While shopping throughout Will County for a day treatment location, Bill Kahoun, the day program director, remembers looking at abandoned supermarkets, strip malls, and "old mansions out in the middle of nowhere" before choosing the bank building. It was the downtown location of the bank, right in the heart of a unique, diverse community, that appealed to the founders. The people served at Lockport Center frequent the antique stores and local restaurants during their spare time. They walk down the busy street and are continually reminded that they are not alone fighting the persistent voices accompanying schizophrenia, the delusions shadowing a bipolar disorder, or the lack of motivation concurrent with clinical depression. Today, the number of people served has grown from the first handful to more than a hundred, and the agency also serves teenagers diagnosed with both mental illness and a developmental disability. Mike Brown, Harold Hyde, and Tony Rivera are still with the Lockport Center. And Lockport strives to accommodate the growing list of people desiring services and supports.

Images from Within

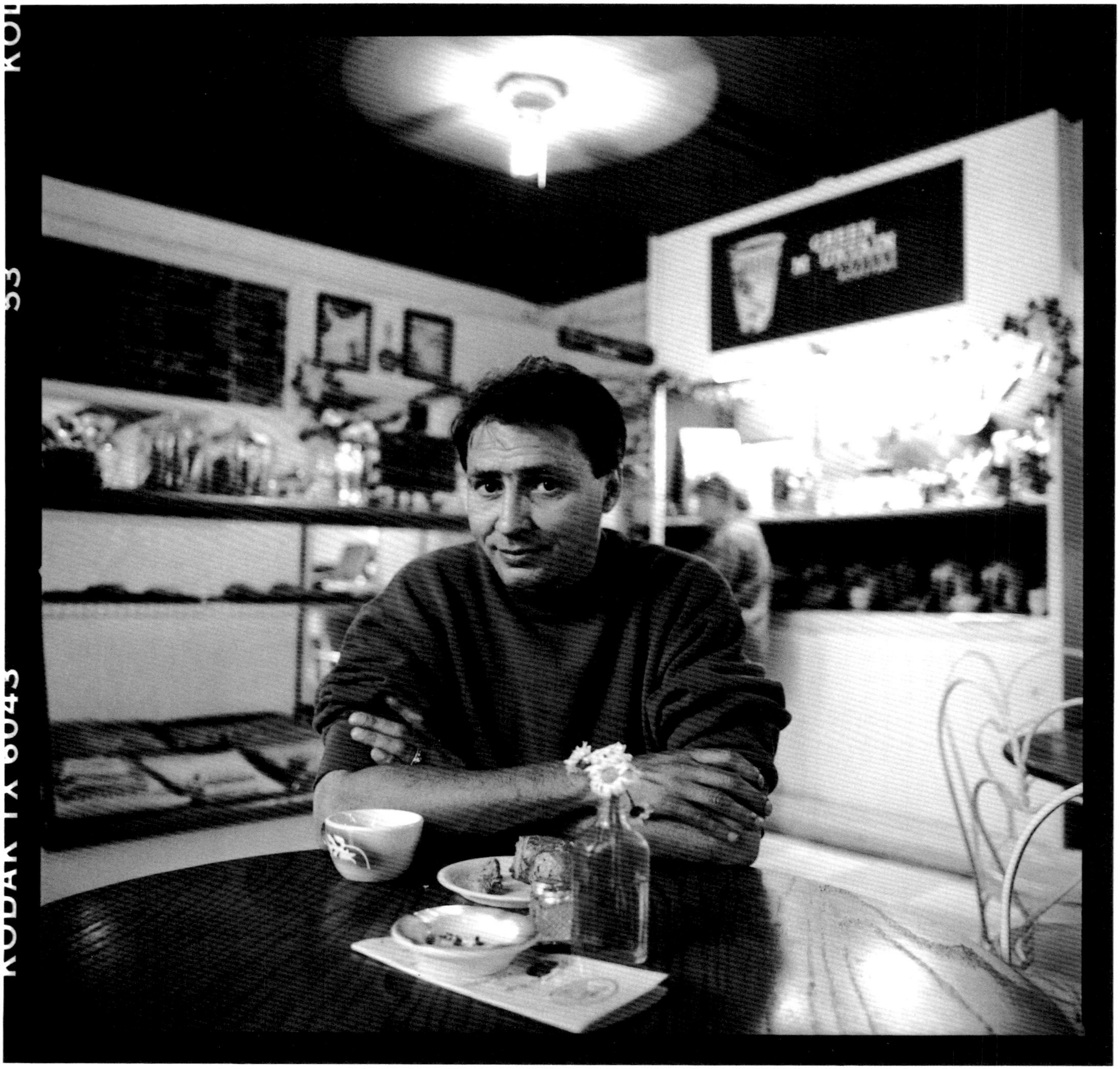
KODAK TX 6043
33

Tony Rivera

Lou's Place gets locked at 11:00 a.m., so I had nowhere to go to get coffee. I started going down to Pastimes Cafe & Antiques with a preacher named Norm. I said to him, "Norm, I have money, I work, why are you doing this?" He said he did it because he likes to.

After Norm left I came in here by myself and ordered a pitcher of coffee. For a while I was in here every week, looking at the clothes and antiques. I wanted to buy this teddy bear Christmas ornament for my mom but it got sold too fast.

It's not too crowded or too loud. When I first came here I told them that their set-up reminds me of the coffee shops out east in Baltimore and Maryland. They laughed and we've been friends for two years. They know my name when I walk in. I used to know all their names but I only come every few weeks now and I can't remember. They make me feel comfortable, like I'm not bothering anybody.

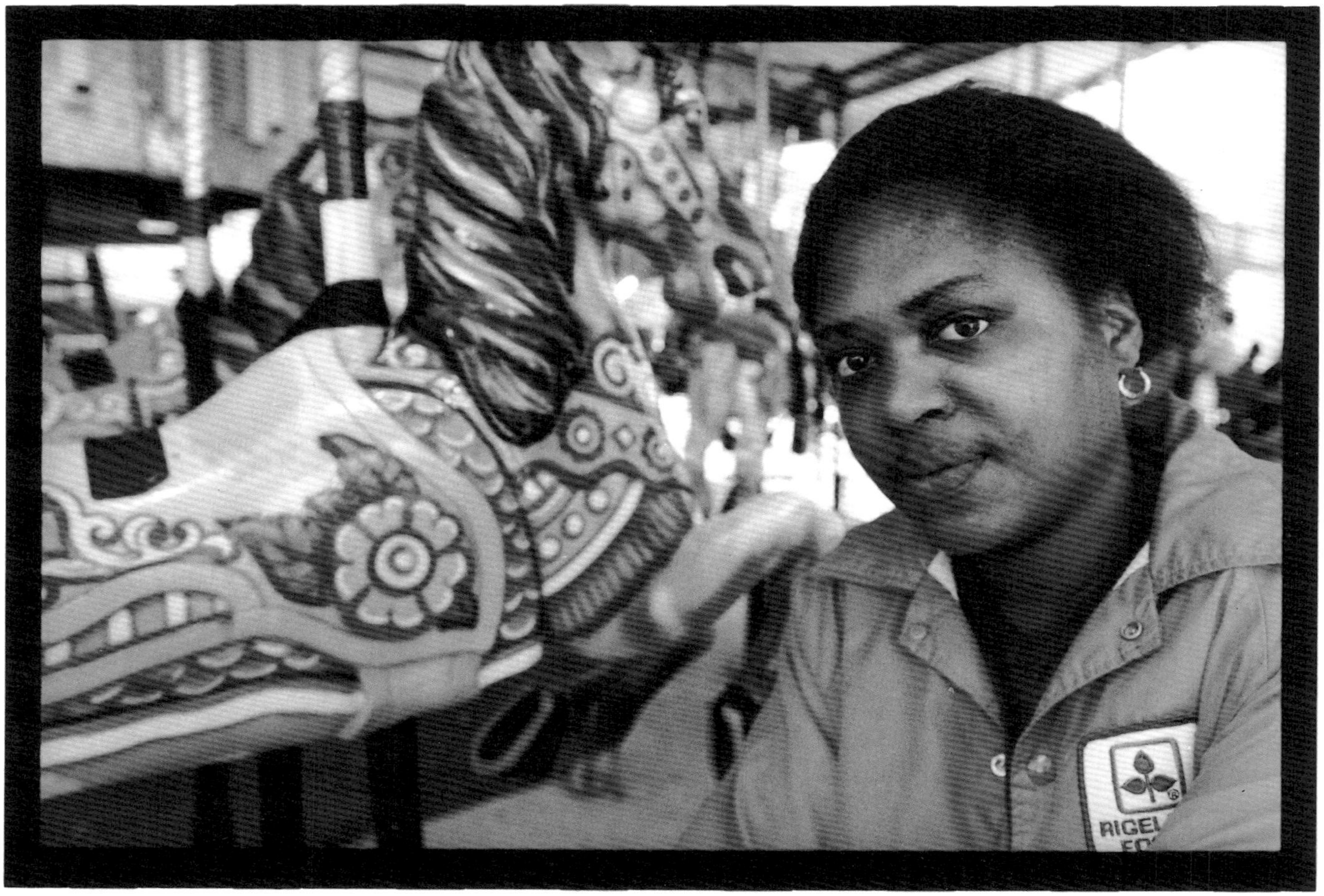

Patti Reid

Seeing other people makes me happy. Kids walking, visiting with my brothers, and watching people snow ski on television also make me happy.

I just came to Lockport. I used to live in a house with my family, but I have a rare disorder which makes me think about the past. In 1992 I got this disorder and I couldn't drive my car anymore. I miss driving the most.

My two big battles are smiling and taking my medications. Both of these are very hard.

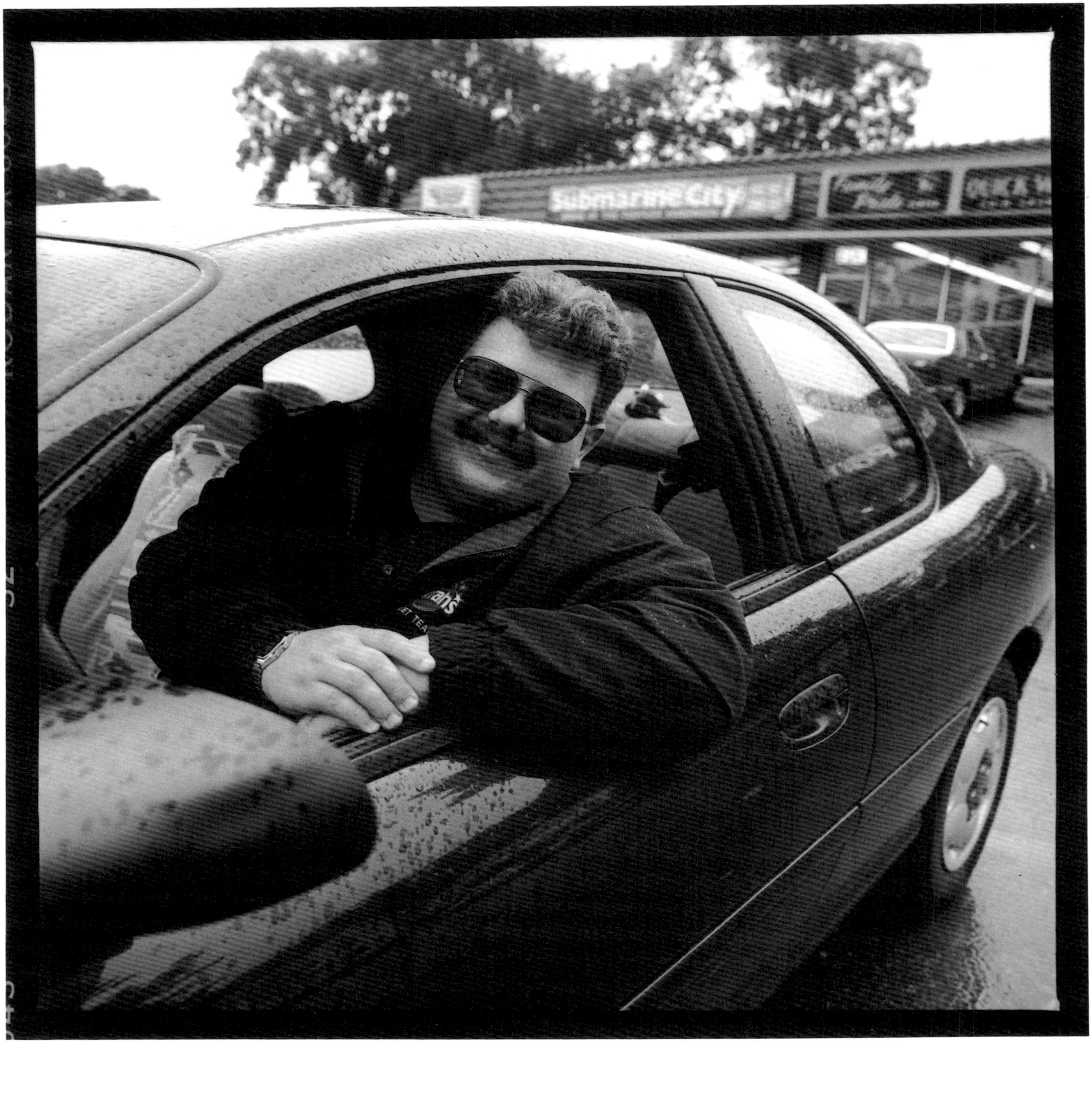
Submarine City

William Wisniowski

There's nothing better than living in your own world — maybe because I'm safe in that world, maybe because I'm well liked in my world that I belong in. Who knows? I want to succeed and live a normal life again like I was before I got sick or ill.

When I graduated from Romeoville High School in 1991 I was voted Most Outstanding Senior of my special services class. I felt terrific about all the work I had accomplished. It wasn't easy because there had been some bad times throughout high school. I suffered depression but didn't take any medication for it or anything.

I'm succeeding every day here, and really working on trying to deal with my behaviors and help myself out of depression. I go to groups every day, and especially like Stinkin' Thinkin', Anger Management, Creative Writing, and Assertiveness.

I live in Romeoville with my parents and drive to Lockport every day. My car is my pride and joy.

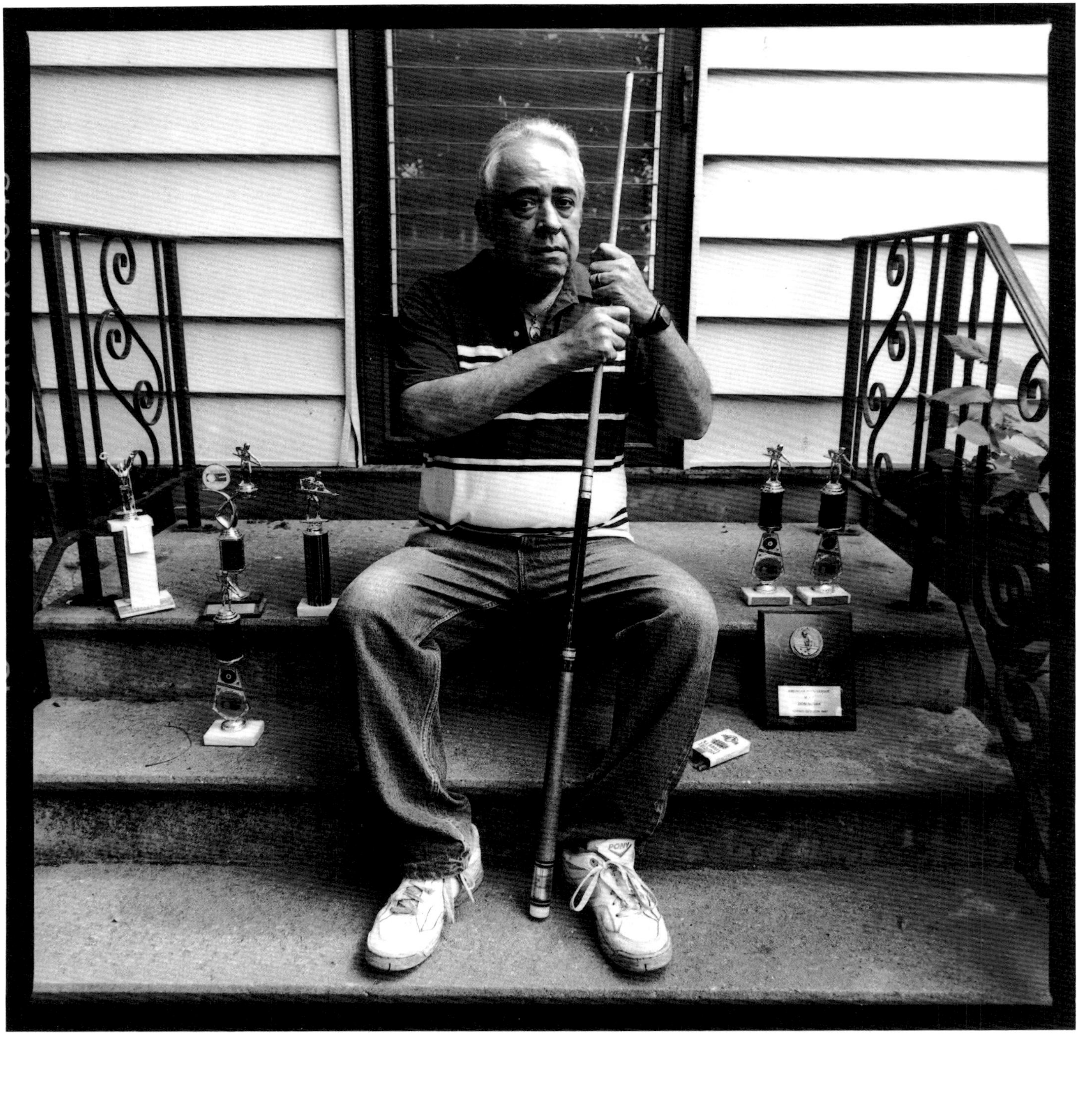

Don Novak

To get into a pool hall in 1959 you had to be sixteen years old. I was fourteen at the time and my brother was seventeen. He used to bring me to a pool room in the back of Olivo's Barber Shop in Joliet.

Just two weeks after I learned how to play, I was beating my brother and a lot of other people, too.

We grew up in an Italian neighborhood in Joliet on the south side, in a house my mother inherited. My dad was fifty-seven years old when I was born and my mother was forty-two — it was a change in life, sort of surprise for them. They didn't think my mom could have children anymore.

I was first diagnosed with schizophrenia. They later changed it to manic depression. I was one of the first patients on the floor of St. Joe's psych ward in 1963. They had just opened. I got five shock treatments that first week, one a day. It erased my memories. I had a lot of bad memories, so it was a good thing. It took the pain of the memories away.

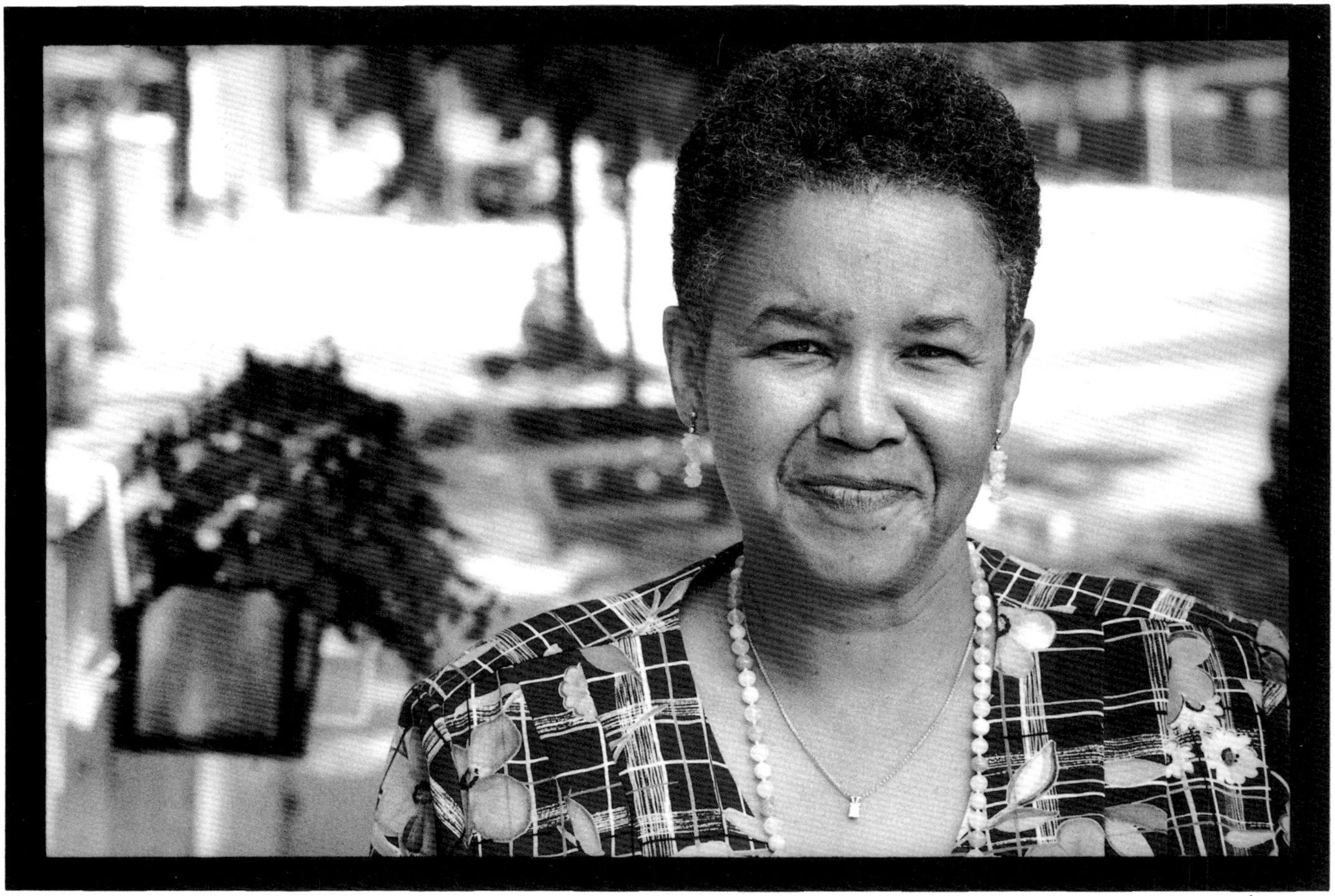

Sharon Parker

The fifty women in Unit Two had not bathed for six or seven months. Viola, or "the woman who gossiped too much," was sent to her first institution in the 1920s and appeared to have no mental illness. Sylvie, the European woman, wrapped herself around toilets and required staff to pull her away. The pacing woman called for Christ all day long while another woman answered her.

On a summer morning in 1969, Sharon Parker became supervisor of Unit Two despite the echoes of friends and colleagues who questioned her move to Elgin State Mental Hospital. They told her she wouldn't like it.

Bathing all the women in the unit seemed like the most obvious way to begin working with them. Parker's suggestion was greeted by laughter from the staff, who had not been supervised in a long time. Their smirks made it clear they weren't going to respect twenty-two-year-old Parker or her ideas for improvement.

At her next encounter with her staff, Parker wore a patient's gown, a bathing cap, and rubber shoes. She once again requested help with gathering the women and assembling them into a long line. One by one, she washed each woman. Earlier that morning she had obtained new "strong dresses," made of material able to withstand dragging and tearing fits. Inside each rolled up strong dress she had placed underwear and slips — items that some of the women in Unit Two had not worn for decades. She gave each woman a set of the garments.

Parker admits it was a very institutional method of bathing, with all the women standing in line, awaiting their turn. Yet it was more humane than the fire hoses that used to blast roomfuls of patients while simultaneously removing feces from walls and ceilings.

Soon the staff was assisting the women with bathing twice a week. In addition, the women attended tea and coffee parties. Parker instructed them on how to "sit like ladies" and encouraged focused conversations.

When Unit Two closed in 1971, forty of the fifty women were able to leave Elgin. Viola lived out her days in a community, with more material to draw gossip from than in the stagnant state hospital.

I didn't think about what people would say about me. They just needed to be bathed, so that's what I did. Over the past thirty years, I've found that what other people think should never stop you from doing what's right. Now I am on the other end of the continuum, assisting others with fulfilling their dreams in the community.

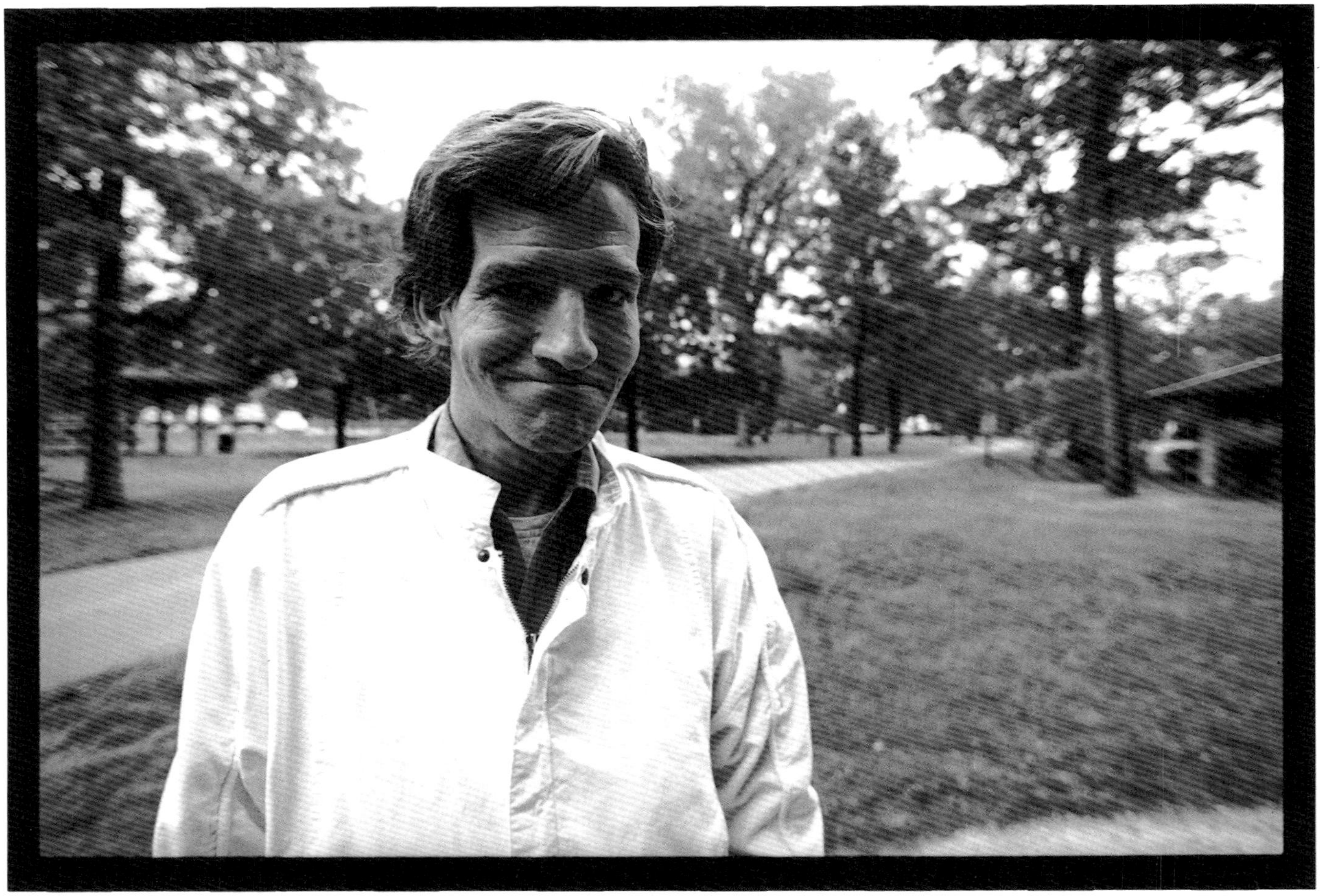

Jim Workman

I'd describe myself as easy going, but I don't like to take too much crap. I can give it, but I just can't take it. I don't like people telling me I can't do something. If you can't get stuff yourself, don't let nobody else get it for you.

I'm thinking about getting a job, talking to Layla [a supported employment counselor] about helping to get me a job. I'd like to do dishwashing. My legs aren't so good but I can lean against the sink.

I don't want no girlfriend. I'm a single man, a bachelor to the hilt. Don't want no married rings.

I want people to know that we're not worthless here, like some think about people with mental illnesses. I get up everyday and come here to Lockport and do as much as I can and what I can. Okay, that's all.

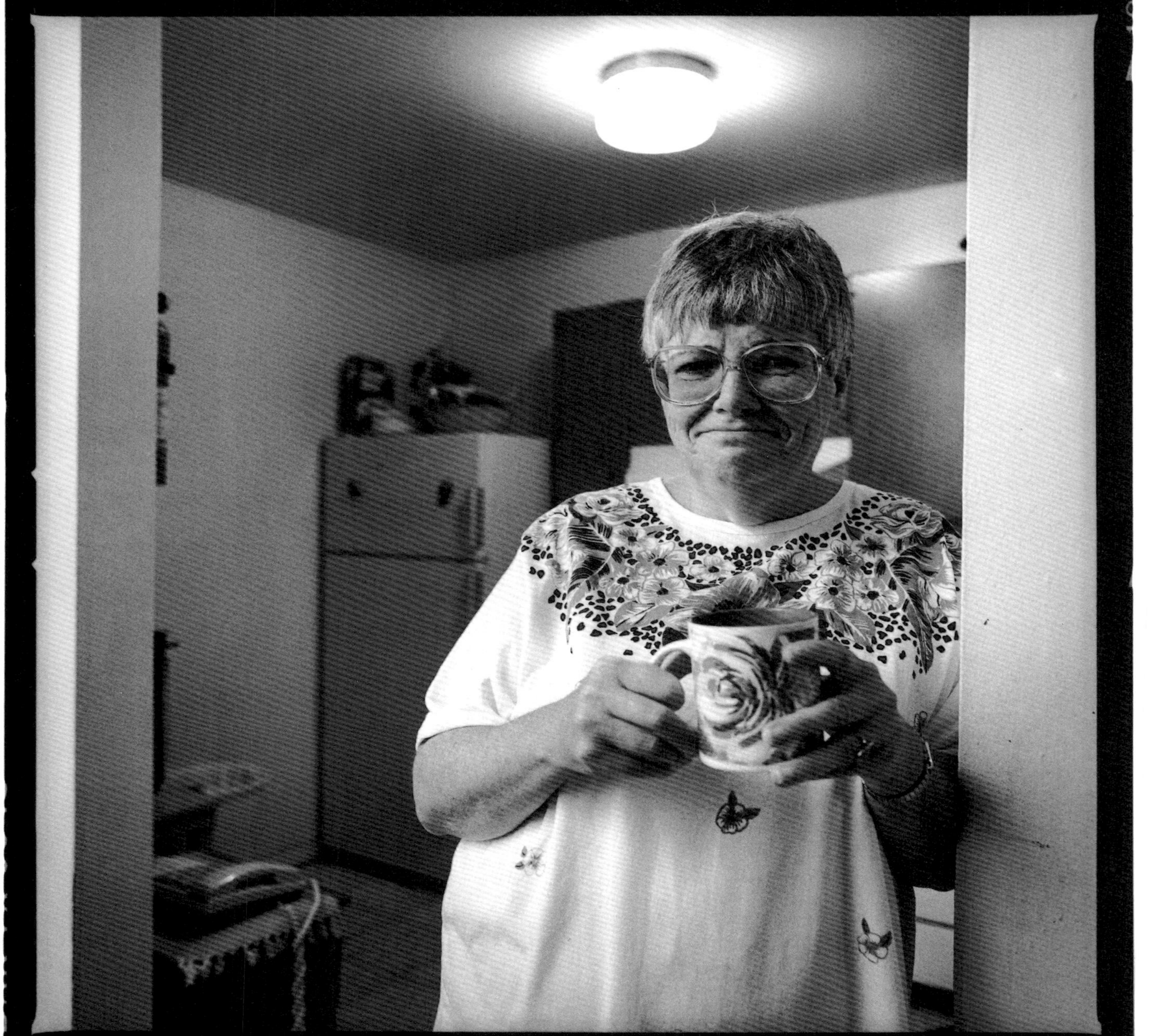

Maureen Daly

Well, I can tell you that I've had a pretty sad life, with going into institutions and hospitals. Institutions, I think, are very militaristic. Everyone has to do what they tell you to do.

Here, things are getting better. You're on your own, it's comfortable. I have my apartment always in order. We've got a dishwasher and my roommate and I take turns cleaning.

I have two children that I've never seen. It has affected my frame of mind, but I know now that I've got to stop blaming people for the problems I've created.

Every day during the week I volunteer an hour at the National Alliance for the Mentally Ill office in Lockport. The woman there is very nice. She will always give me something to do. For a while now I've been rolling up papers for the tag day. The papers explain different types of mental illness, so more people can understand. In the past, the whole approach was, "Be quiet, don't talk about it."

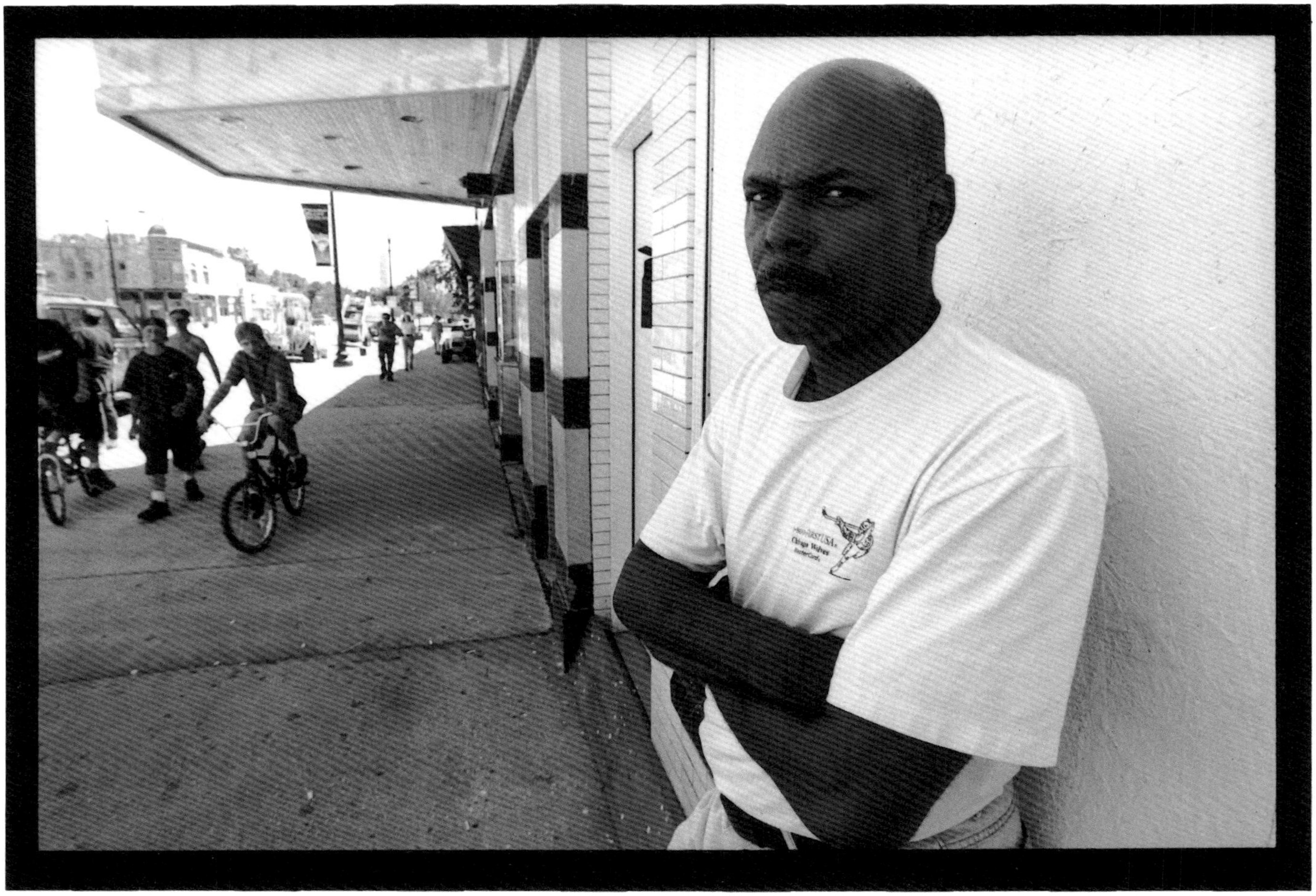

Mike Brown

I like my job, at times. While I'm working I think about all kinds of stuff, like what I'm going to do with my paycheck and private thoughts.

Sharon Parker recruited a bunch of us to come to Trinity in 1991, because our program with Will County was folding. We had a choice to come here, and it sounded better than anywhere else. I like that they were going to find us housing and help out with our medications.

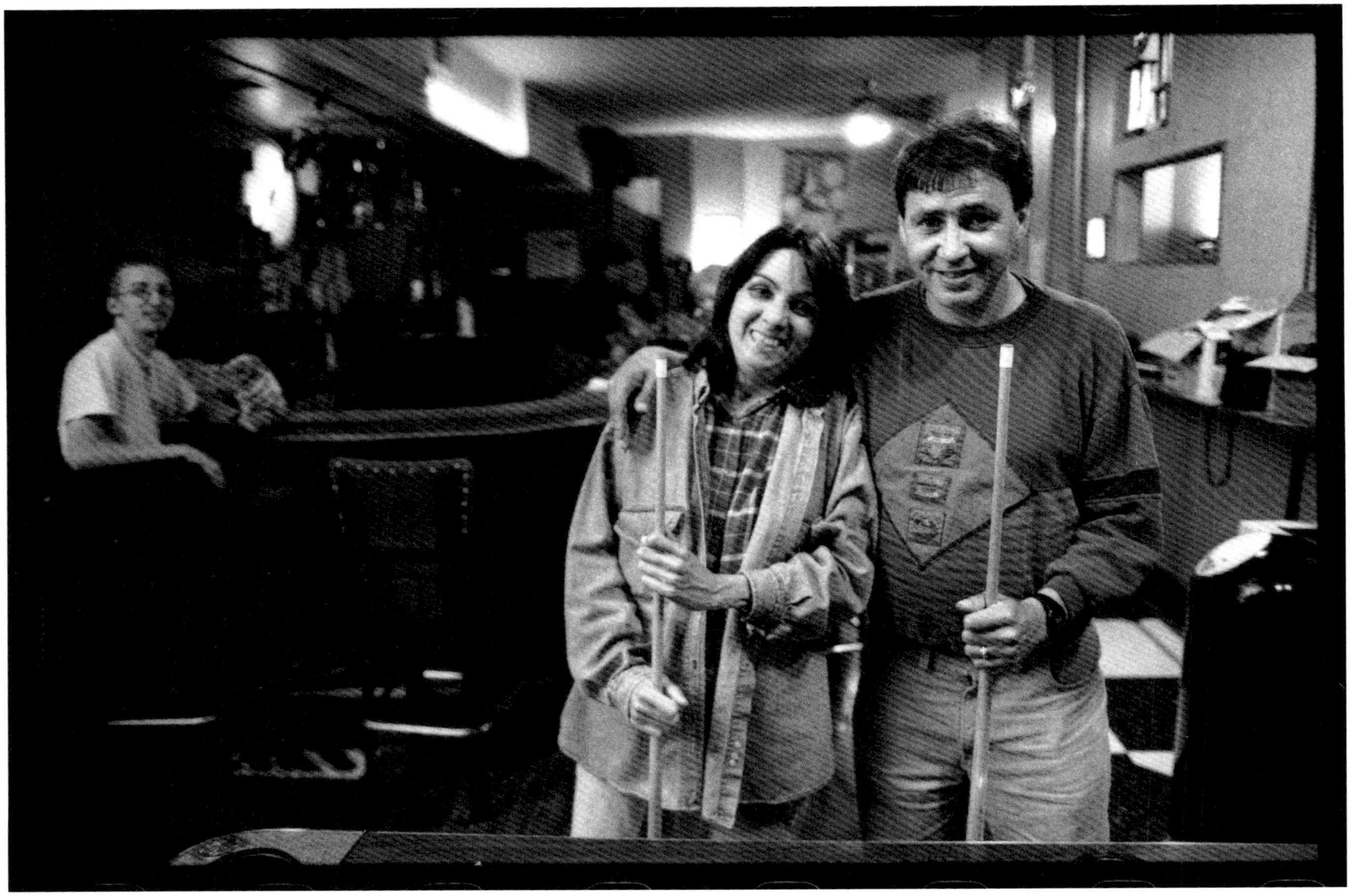

Sue Fencl

Describe myself in three words? I can be nice, nasty, and cruel. But most of all I can be lovable… if I'm not rubbed the wrong way.

I see that there's some people here at Trinity that I remember knowing from other places, like Tinley Park [Mental Health Center]. We go way back. A lot of them haven't changed too much, they're still the same. Me, you could say I'm still the same, but I've grown up a lot. I got a divorce, changed my name back.

My little boy Sammy is ten years old. His nickname is Moe. He's had straight A's since the first grade. My little girl, the four-year-old, she's smart, too. Both of them are going to go somewhere in life. Sammy's been fascinating since he was two. He's a good artist, better than I ever was. They live in Coal City with my ex-husband. I see them on weekends sometimes.

I've overcome the obstacle of not being with my kids. Even when I get out of here I know it's going to take a long period of time before I can be with them. I've got to get a lawyer to see if I'm mentally competent.

I want to change my three words to lovable, wicked, and friendly. I can be your friend if you're not a back-stabber. I have a good relationship with a couple of clients, like Mike Brown and Tony Rivera. We're all close, we're all friends and we go way back. We know each other's limits, and we all sort of forget each other's problems.

I define my problem as trying to get out of here. If I weren't here I'd be trying to go back to Coal City. I'm very concerned about my kids. My husband is taking good care of them, and I won't try to interrupt his life or take over. I just want to be closer to them. I'd try to find a job in Coal City and make friends. Make friends all over again.

Why do I just have men as friends? Well, I was a tomboy when I was little, and I've always hung around guys. I have a mouth on me… a rude, crude mouth. Guys can make me laugh, I can make them laugh. I just get along better with the male sex.

I think Trinity is helping people, like the ones who don't have homes and need counselors. Now other places are cutting back on helping. Tinley Park Mental Health Center has got less staff and it's harder to get in. I like it here in Lockport, and I think it's good that we're on State Street. Though some of us might dress or act weird or function differently or embarrass us, it doesn't matter. That's just how they are, it can't be helped. But they are getting helped, and have a home to stay at.

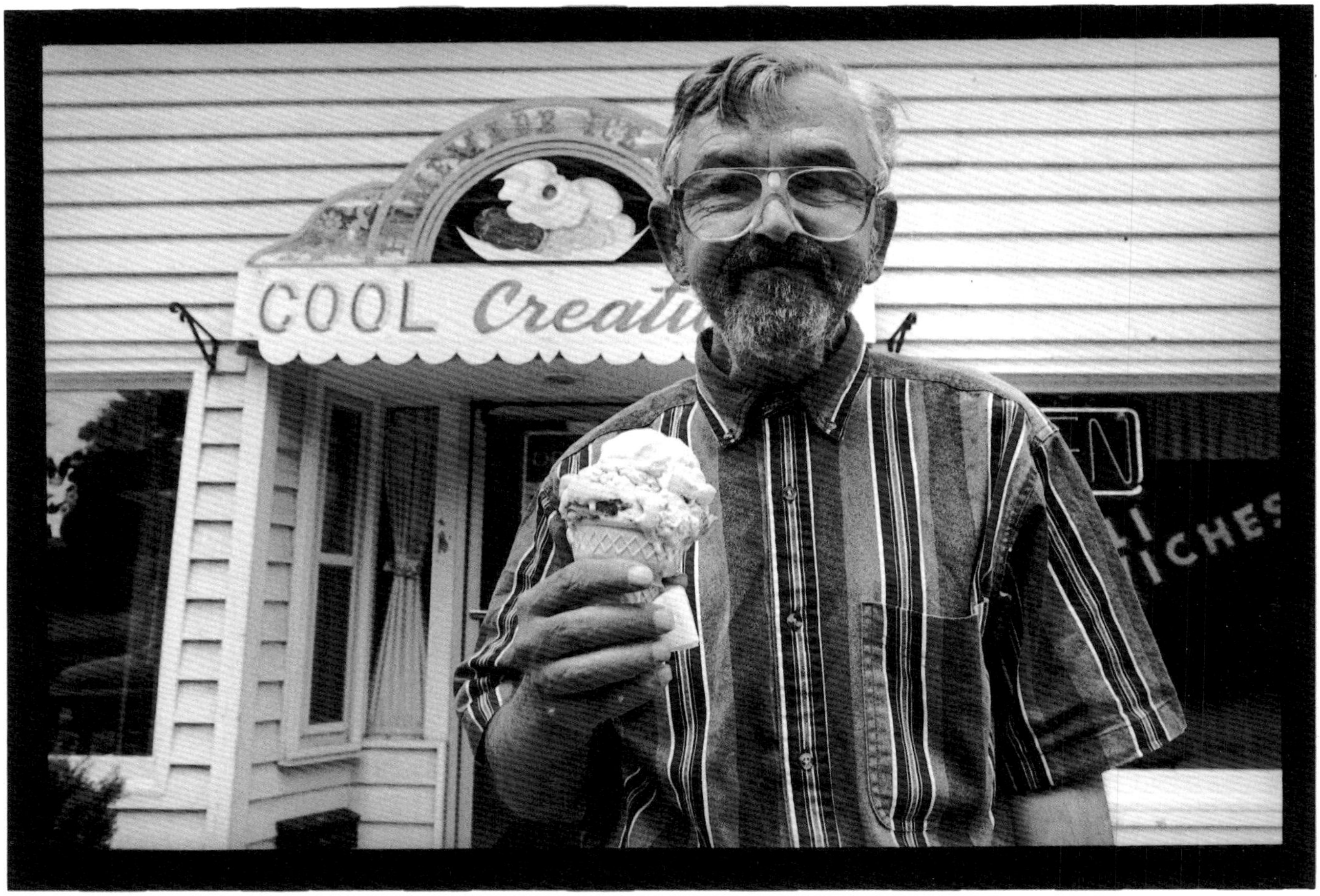
COOL Creati

Harold Hyde

I have one wish. I want Barbara Anne Grendell to come out of heaven so she can marry me. She died in a bathtub at the YMCA. She was twenty-two years old. I wonder if she'd recognize me?

I had a wife-to-be. Her name was Linda and she had black hair. We danced together and roller-skated. She's married to somebody else now. What was the color of her eyes? What kind of question is that? I never really noticed. I was too young to think about those things.

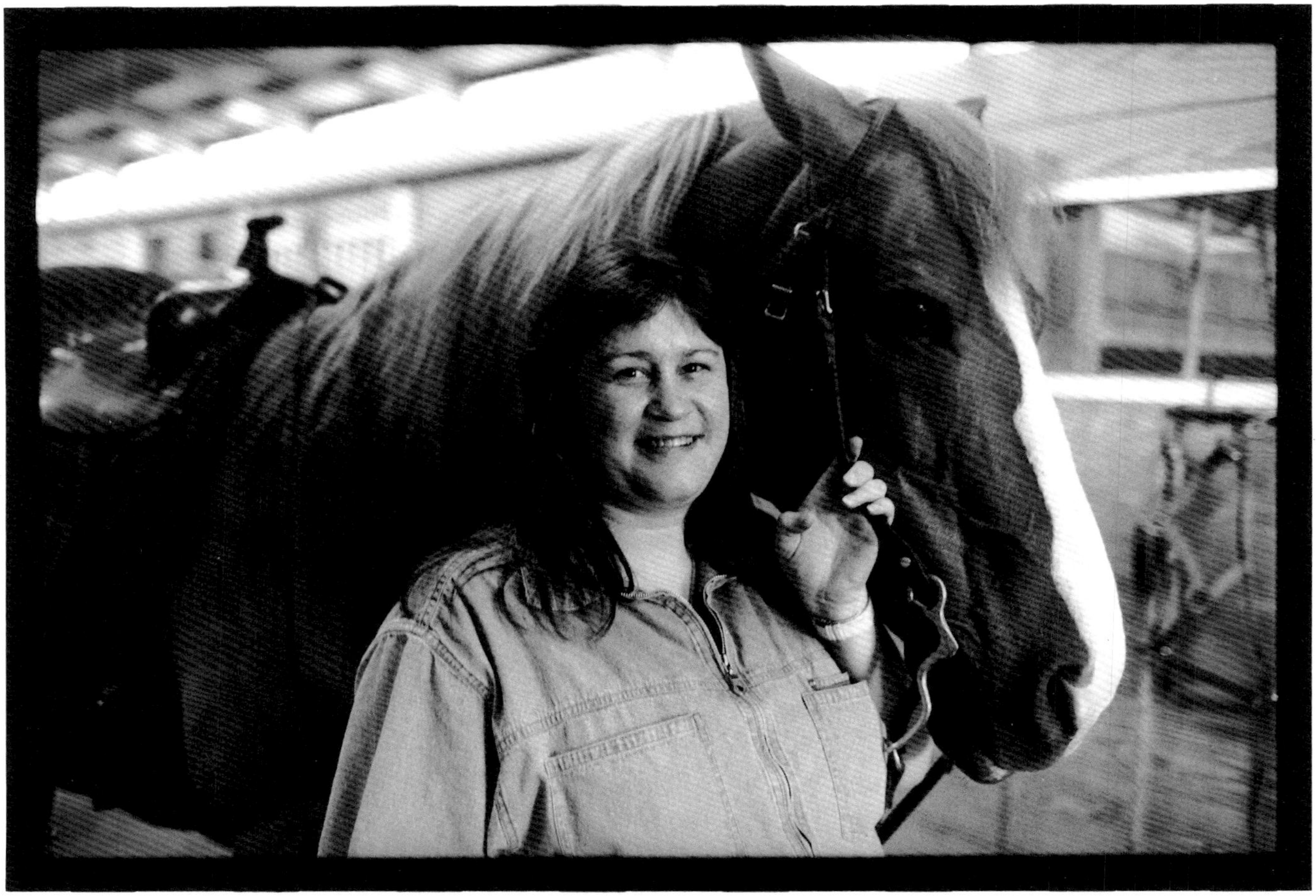

Diane Gaglione

The first time I tried to go horseback riding at Strides, I was scared and nervous. It had been a long time since I rode a horse, and I was wondering if I could use telepathy on the horse to calm us both down. Bill Kahoun helped me with that and explained you can't use telepathy on horses. He helped me get on Flash, and it was the greatest thing I could have ever achieved. I really owe it all to him.

On May 17, 1998 I entered a 4-H competition and won a first place blue ribbon and trophy. They are sitting on top of my television.

I'm still nervous when I walk into Strides every Wednesday. But I just go up to Flash, give him a big hug and kiss and he knows it's me. After a little while I feel comfortable enough to trot and cantor. Horseback riding is great exercise for me. It's like you develop a relationship with the horse and get a high from it. It's a high on life.

Strides is a stable in Lockport Township that is devoted to therapeutic horseback riding. Along with the people served by Trinity, the stable serves individuals with disabilities from other organizations and the community.

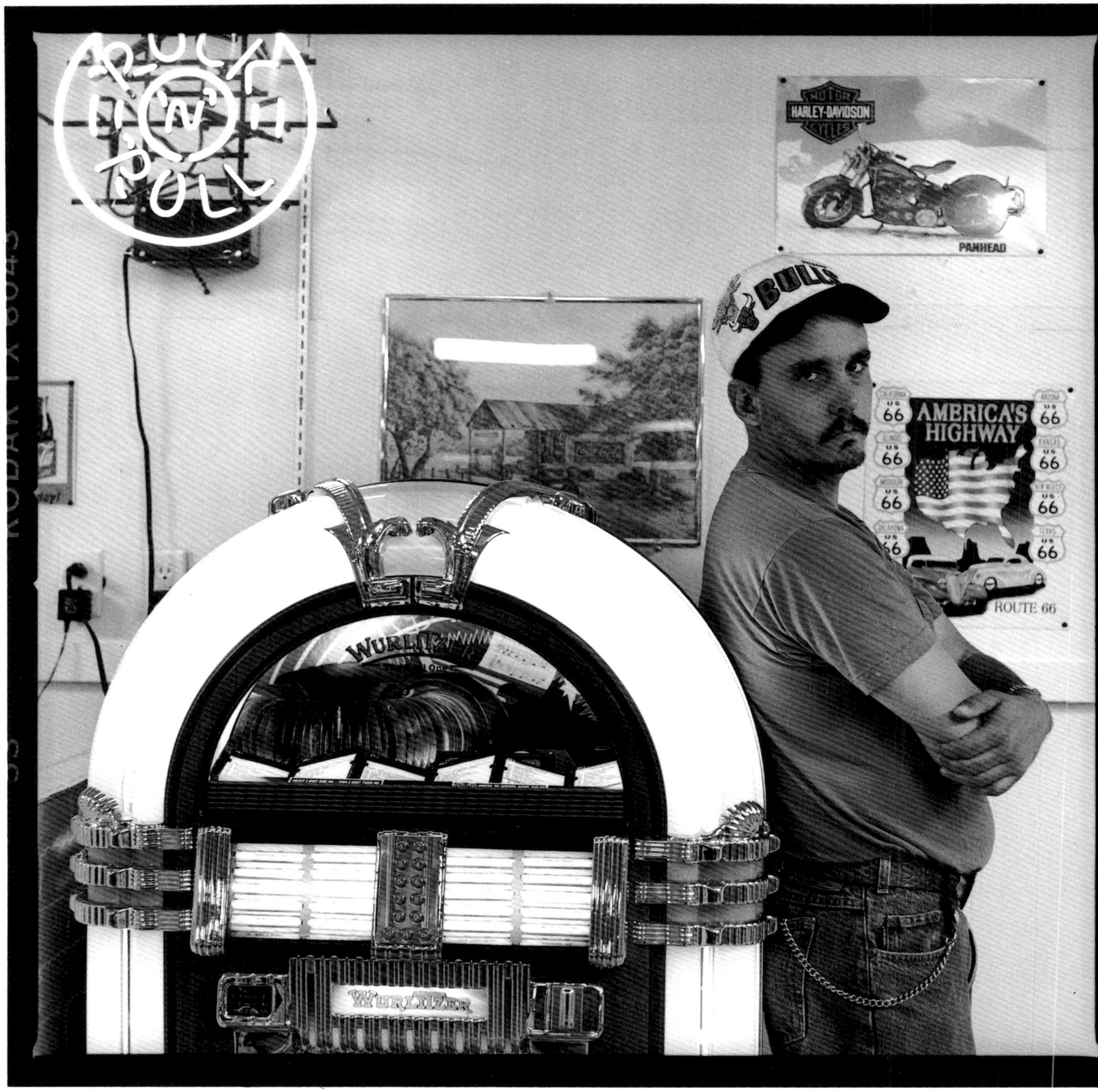
ROCK 'N' ROLL
HARLEY-DAVIDSON
MOTOR CYCLES
PANHEAD
BULLS
AMERICA'S HIGHWAY
ROUTE 66
WURLITZER
WURLITZER
KODAK TX 6043
35

Ross Price

I was raised and brought up on a farm in Arkansas. We had to get up early, feed the animals, walk two miles to school and two miles back. In the summers and fall it wasn't so bad, but the winters, man. Don't get me started on the winters.

A few years ago I lost over two hundred pounds. All I did was eat all day long, like I just finished dinner and would go to the store to eat more junk food before bed. Finally I got sick of being so fat and stopped eating greasy foods and cutting back on food. I'm a lot healthier now. I got a job with a landscaping company. I love working outside. I can't stay cramped up indoors all day.

My goals in life are to continue landscaping and stay focused on the job, try to stay out of psychiatric hospitals for depression, hearing voices, suicidal thoughts. Most of the people that I'm around who have never been in psychiatric hospitals don't understand. I walked into a store and they were like, "Here comes that schizo fruitcake." You know, I just let it go in one ear and out the other. Because if you don't, the whole world will build up on you and you'll lose your temper and go off more.

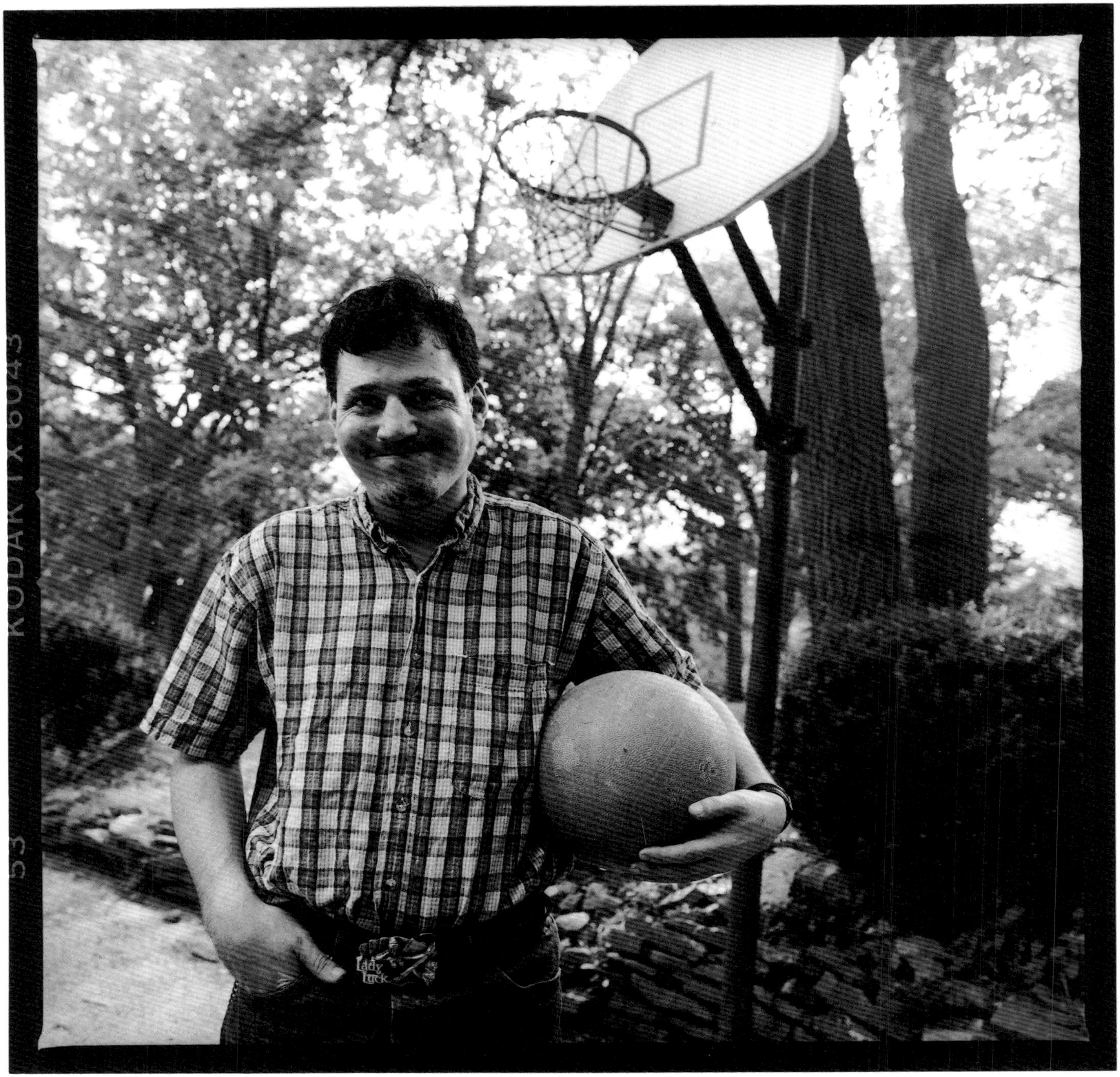
KODAK TX 6043
53
Lady Luck

Greg Giannini

I'd describe myself as a regular person.

I started out in a locked up place. It was like if you screwed up with staff then they would put you down in restraints. If you would try to fight they would hurt your arm.

The second place was a little bit different. If you did something there they would just hold you down for a couple of minutes. It hurt. It made me feel like they had more power than I did.

Here they haven't done any of that stuff to me.

I wish that I could be living on my own. I'm not trying to do again what I did at my other job, which was run away from it. Now I don't have a job anymore.

Most of the time I like taking walks around my house. Before I was living in a group home out in the country, and you don't have that many stores or streets to walk on. I like walking to 7-Eleven and Mr. D's fast food.

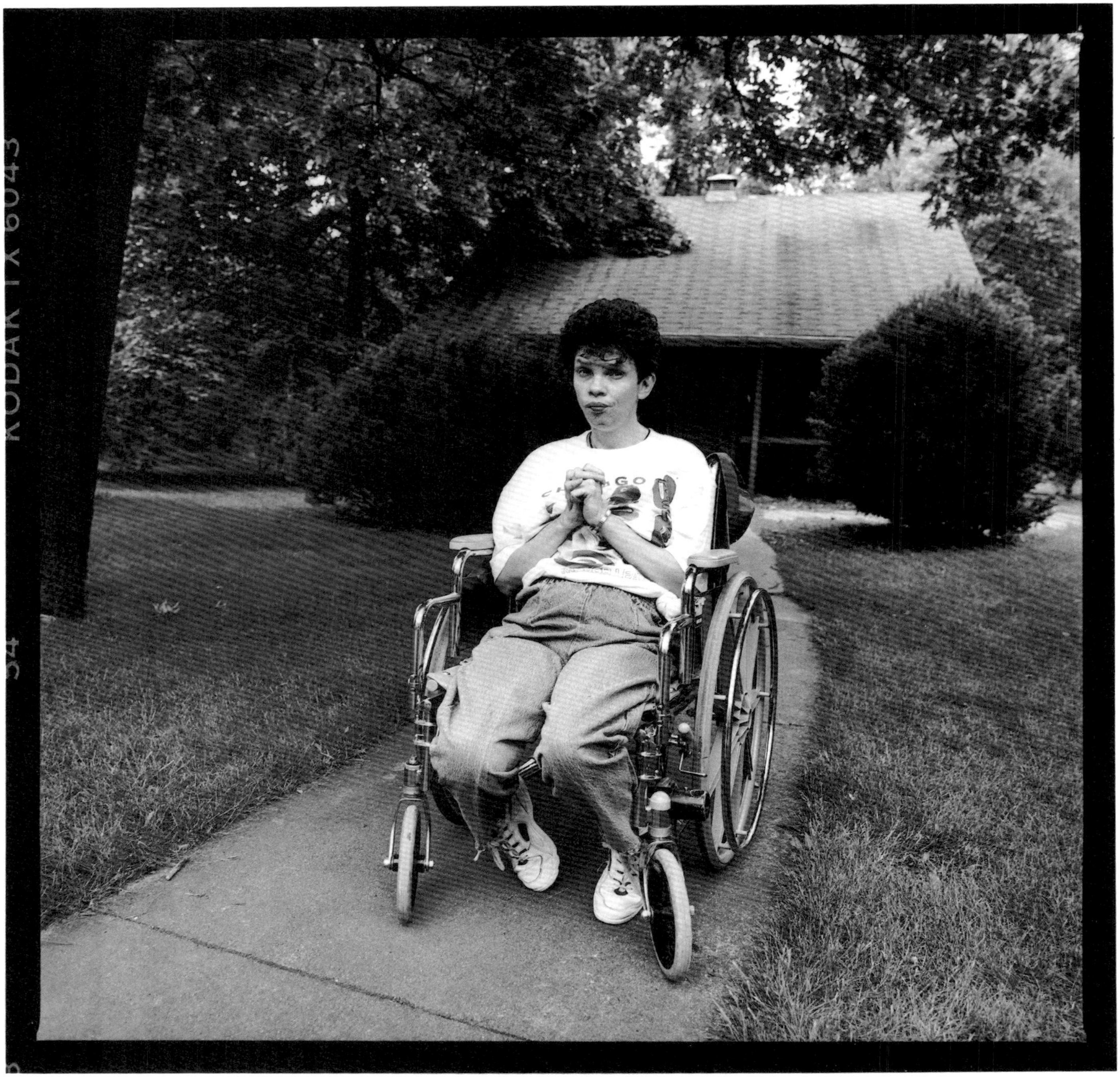

Pam Chenault

I think people are thinking, "There goes a retarded person," when they see me on the street. If I could say something to them I would tell them that I am normal. People look down on me somehow because I'm disabled and I don't want to be looked down on like that. I am a forty-year-old woman with cerebral palsy and a behavioral problem. Every day I need to remind myself to stay calm. Trinity has really helped me with my anger. Three years ago I was beating on people and ripping their clothes.

Some of my interests are watching baseball, basketball, and the Home Shopping Network. I don't order anything. I just watch.

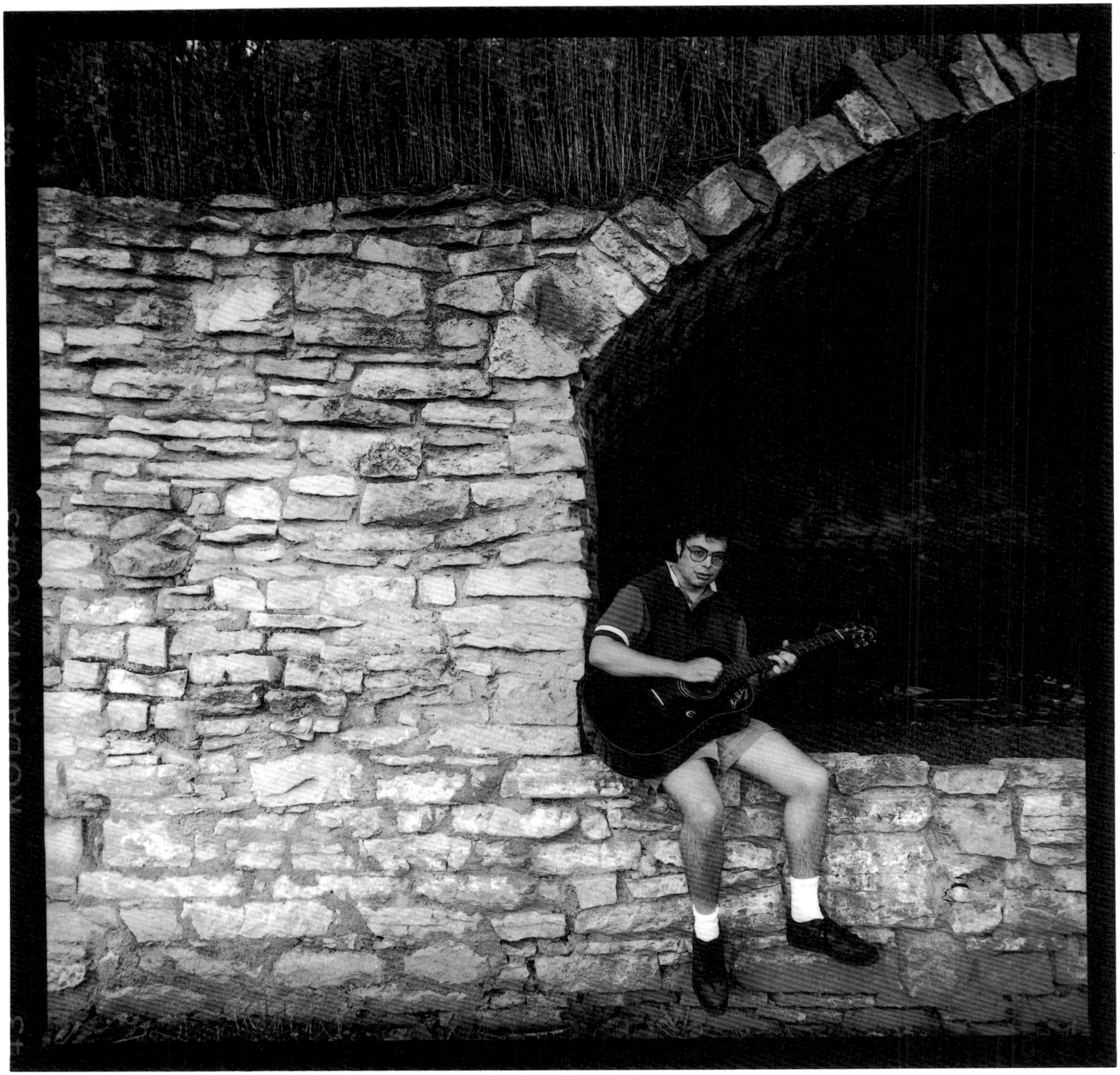

Andrew Arthurs

Playing the guitar helps me pass the time. If there's a party you can just pick it up and sing along. At St. Joe's Hospital last year I played B-I-N-G-O was his Name-O for everyone on the psychiatric floor. It turned into a group sing along. Even the nurses were singing Christmas carols.

I've been studying the Kabbala since 1992. I learned it from an old Jewish man named Marcus. I'm also Jewish. The Kabbala is basically a way of life. It's wisdom, sheer wisdom, wisdom of the ages, wisdom and spiritual facts, as well as things about the world. It's the glowing face of the messiah. I believe The Kabbala proves that there are actions we have to right this world's wrongs. We can each set an example to prove that there is a God who spreads kindness and mercy everywhere.

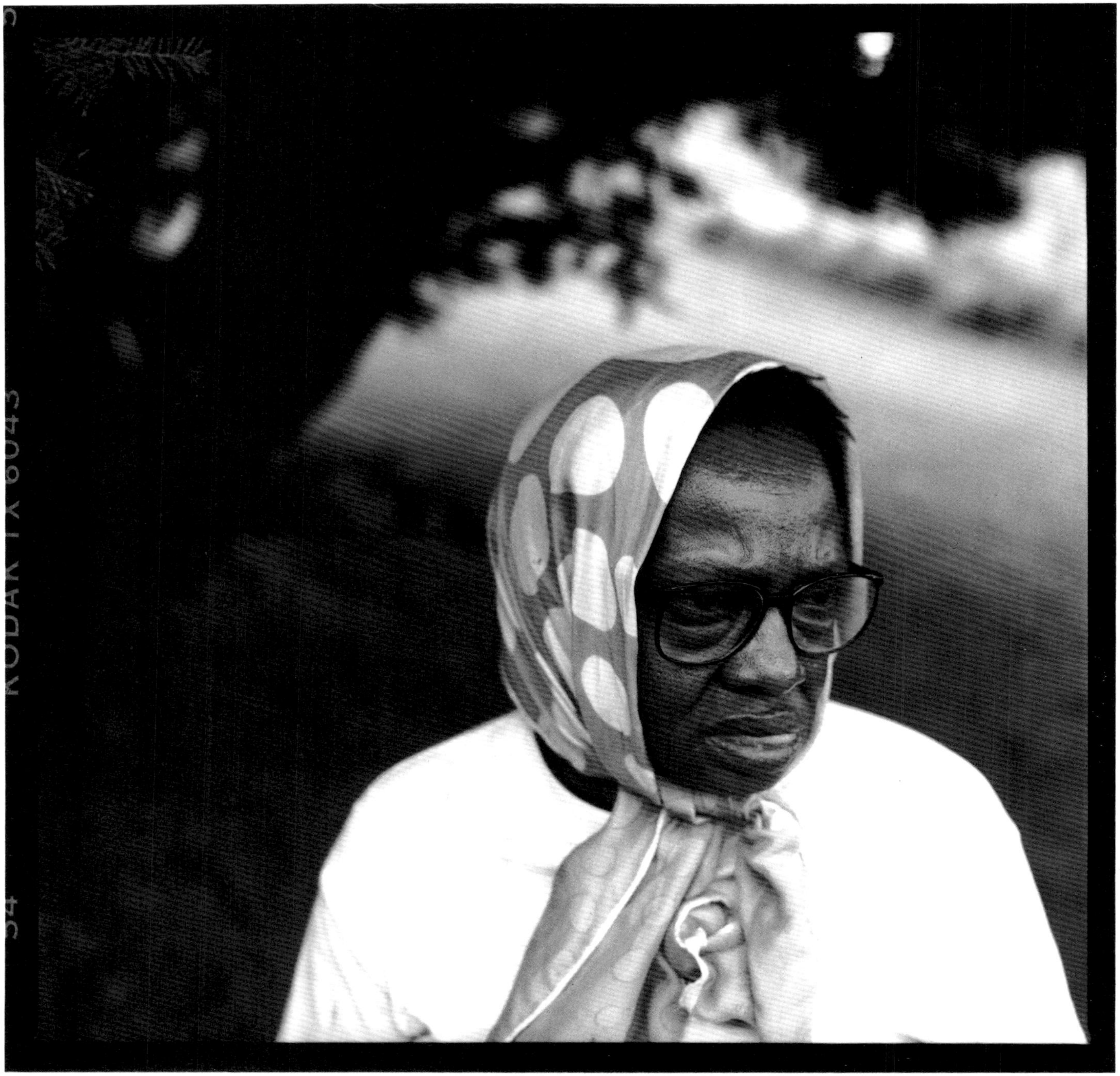
KODAK TX 6043
34

Patsy Sims

I'm the oldest one here at my house. This tree in the backyard is very pretty, wide, and tall. These are expensive trees, and probably cost well over one hundred dollars.

I'd describe myself as a small town person, a hick kind of person. The city is too fast paced for me. There's too much going on in the city all at one time.

What I want people reading this to know is that the staff here is working to get me on the right track, making sure that I'm showering every day, taking pills, and not indulging in too much sugar. I appreciate their efforts. Sometimes I get a little grouchy. I've been here three years and my sugar level has come down considerably. As for any kind of mental illness, I believe I have conquered it. I'm taking my meds, getting enough rest, and not getting into scraps with anyone.

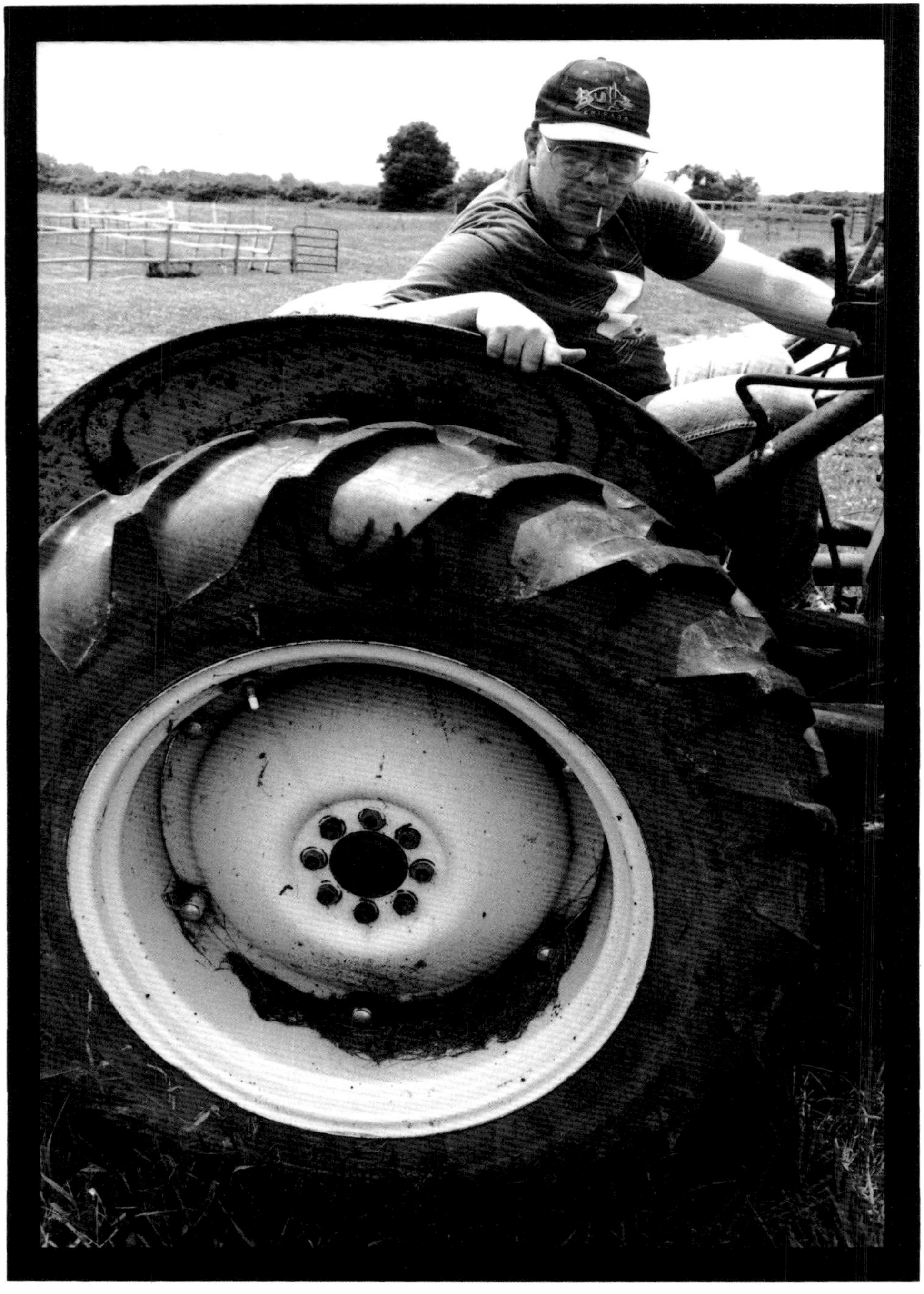

Paul Miller

What's in your mouth?

Oh, it's a piece of straw. It's a habit that I have basically picked up because I was outside and saw some straw. It's something for me to do if I don't have a cigarette.

Are you trying to quit smoking?

No!

Do you work on this tractor?

No, it's an old piece of junk. but it's nice to sit on.

What do you enjoy doing?

I like seeing Phil every day. He's a cool guy and he'll do a lot of things for you. He makes his groups fun. It doesn't have to be serious all the time.

Also, I like listening to music, like Eric Clapton tapes. There's this one song about the clouds and the rain but I can't remember the name.

What make you happy?

Pretty girls, if you want to know the truth.

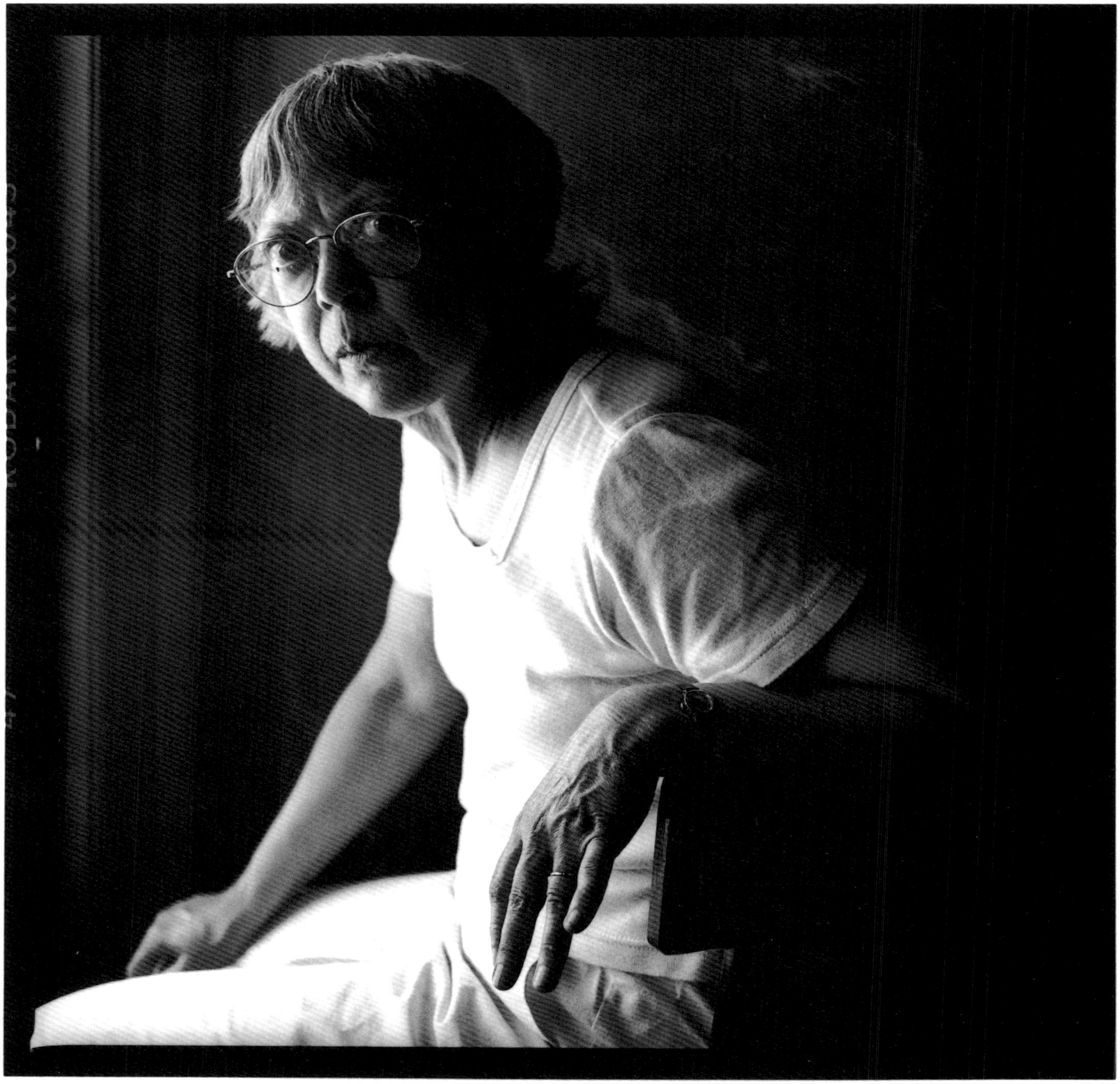

Sylvia McCure

It's OK to be a failure
in one thing
and try something else.
It's OK to be a failure,
just try something else.

Just find someone
anyone, anywhere
and continue your life
whether it be up, down
or on the downward spiral
or on the upward plain
or on the middle plain
or on the lower middle plain.
Be humble.
Be humble when people treat you badly
or act badly, when they hurt you or
when they are upset, when they doubt you,
when they claw you. Just hide somewhere,
heal and medicate.

Sylvia received a bachelor's degree in Social Work with a minor in English Literature from the University of Wisconsin-Madison in 1966. She composed this free verse poem during a creative writing group in the Roxy basement. The focus of the assignment was to write about your personal philosophies.

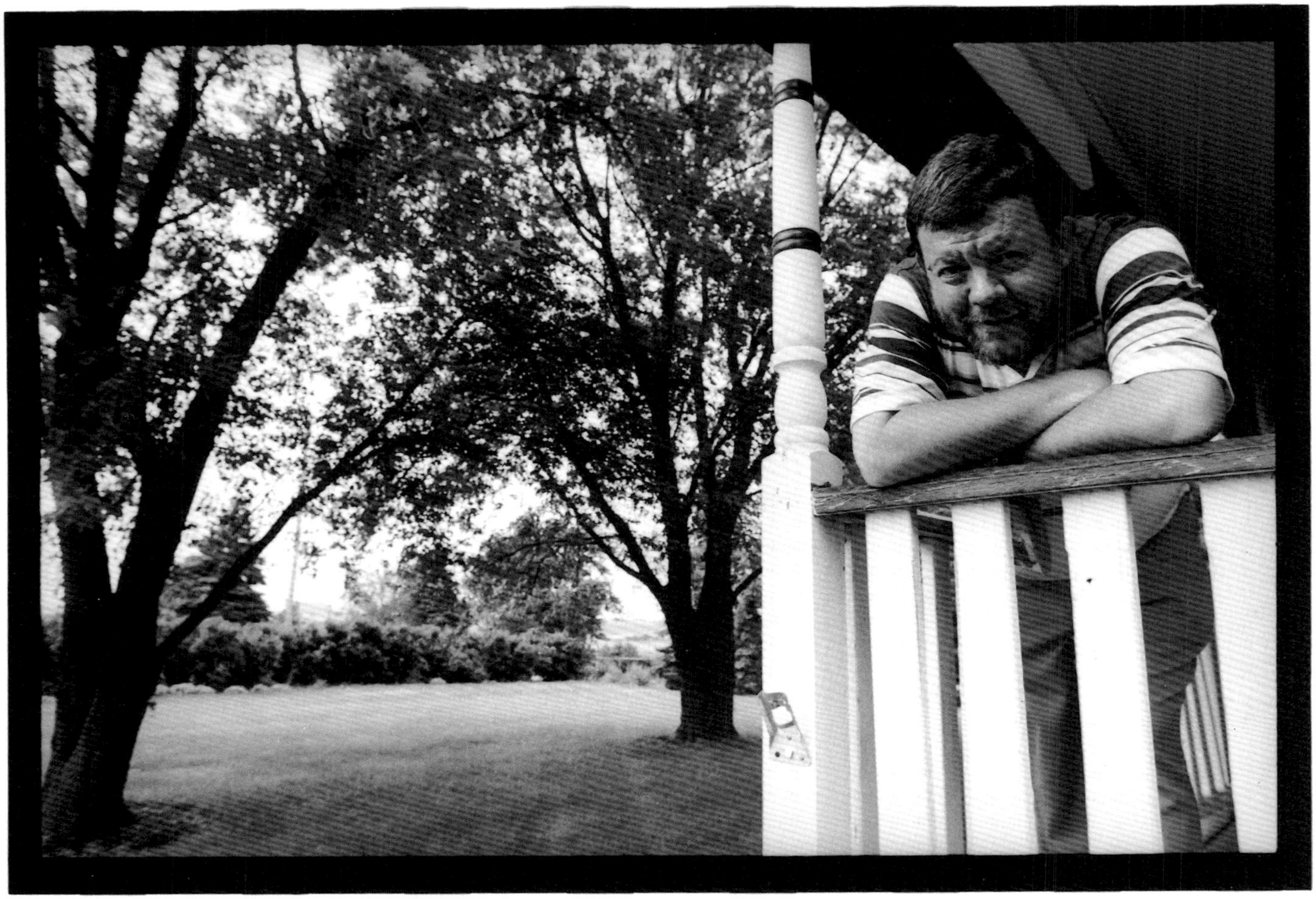

Harold Leyerle

It's really unexplainable. I can get into a book, and it's like I'm there. I can relate to the characters, what they're thinking, experiencing, the setting, the plot.

Reading for me is something that came about in the past couple of years. Before I didn't enjoy reading, and it wasn't relaxing to me. My favorite book is *The Rise and Fall of the Third Reich* by William Shirer. It's 1480 pages of history written from the German side. Shirer takes Hitler's life and brings up what he was all about. You get into his mind and his rise to power. Shirer portrays Hitler as he really was — an evil man who used all of his energies to rise himself up. I just read *The Rise and Fall* a second time and noticed a lot of things I didn't before. I suppose you could read it twenty times and not digest the full impact.

The porch here is great for reading. It's serene, quiet, peaceful. The wind rustles in the trees, the birds chirp. Occasionally I can hear cars driving by on the road. It's picturesque. I always read on this porch.

I was in the Air Force for eight years and graduated from Florida International University. I worked on the F-4E Phantom Jet, a bomber plane. I worked on this aircraft from the time I entered the Air Force, and then went to the Colorado Lowry Training Base in Denver to teach the system to other pilots.

I can empathize with people. I don't think it's a natural quality, it's something you have to work on to develop. I'm an easy person to talk to, and I try to be friendly and outgoing. I think it comes from being a teacher. You have to be concerned about people and their progress more than your own.

I came to Trinity five years ago. My condition was pretty good, but I had experienced bouts of depression at times. I first lived in an apartment with Tony Rivera. After a while, the apartment became too much for me to handle and I moved to a group home on Route 53 in Joliet. There, I learned the importance of cooking, cleaning, and doing other chores. At Trinity at this time, there was a smaller group of clients. With a smaller group, you have closer relationships, and different dynamics.

The attitudes about mental health are much better now than twenty-five years ago. Anyone with a mental illness was labeled a lunatic or a crazy person. Today we're more accepting of people with disabilities.

Now I accept myself as a person with a disability. It was difficult for me to do this in the past. Each day goes by and I do better than the one before. I'm making progress.

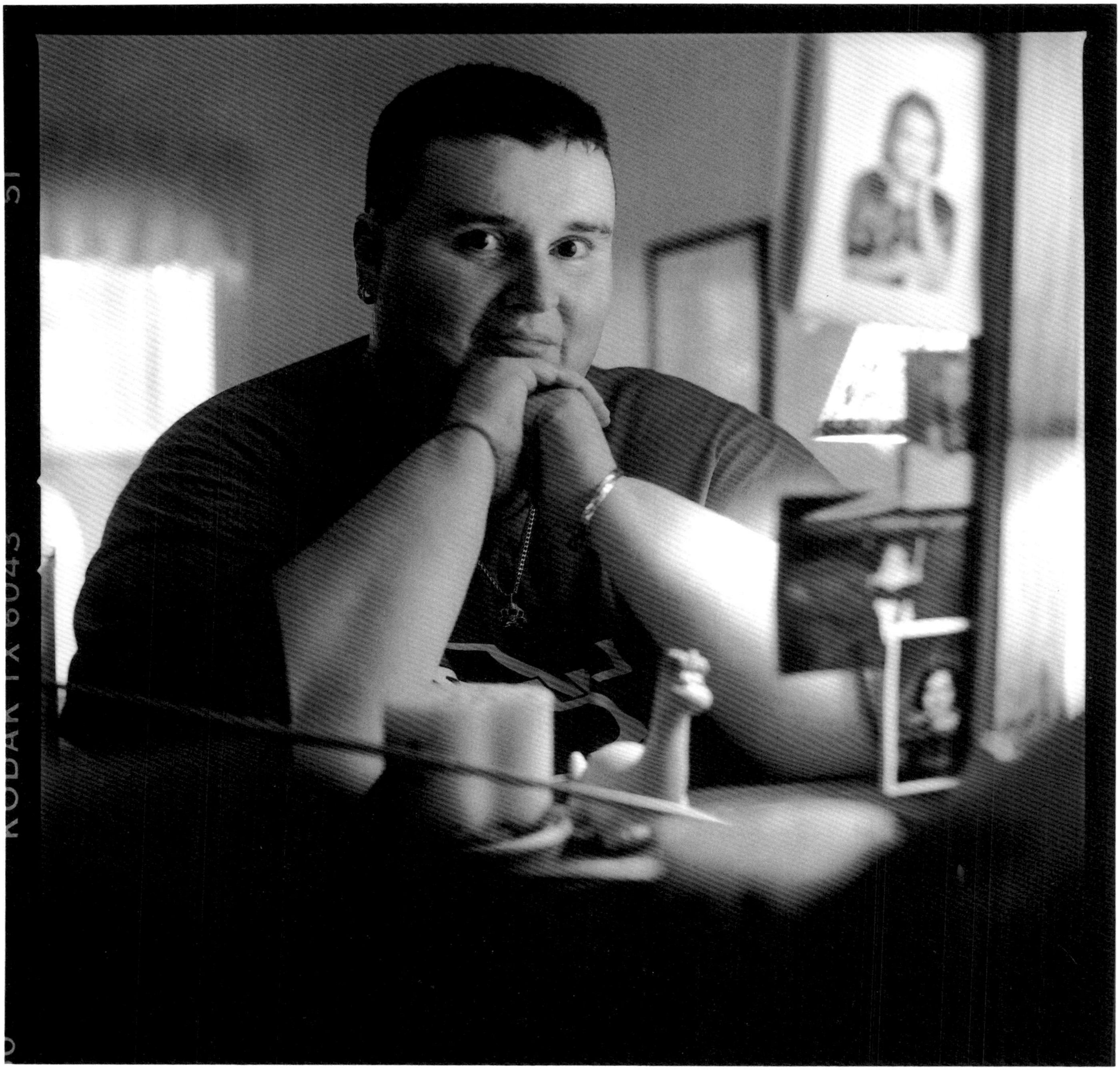
KODAK TX 6043
51

Kathy Molyneaux

I didn't know I was depressed until after college. I just thought everyone felt the same way I did, with the depression. There were problems sleeping, feeling down, overwhelmed, worried, and not happy. My graduation from DePaul University in 1983 was a good day.

After college, I worked successfully as a nurse for thirteen years. I worked at Mercy Hospital, Tinley Park Mental Health Center, and Charter Hospital. I felt like I could relate to the patients, because I had been there myself. I gave out medications and led some groups.

I never figured my problems would get that bad. I never dreamed I'd get to the point where I wasn't able to work.

When I first came here a year ago, I didn't like it. I was used to being independent and having a car. You have to rely on staff to drive you places and can't come and go as you please.

We all have our struggles in this house, but I like it much better now. One of my goals is to enter a master's of counseling program at a local university. I already went back to Governors State University and received a master's in substance abuse counseling. I think I'd maybe like to be an occupational therapist someday. They get to do all the cool things in the hospital, like making and painting ceramics, and other fun stuff with the patients. The nurse just gets to make sure everyone is still alive.

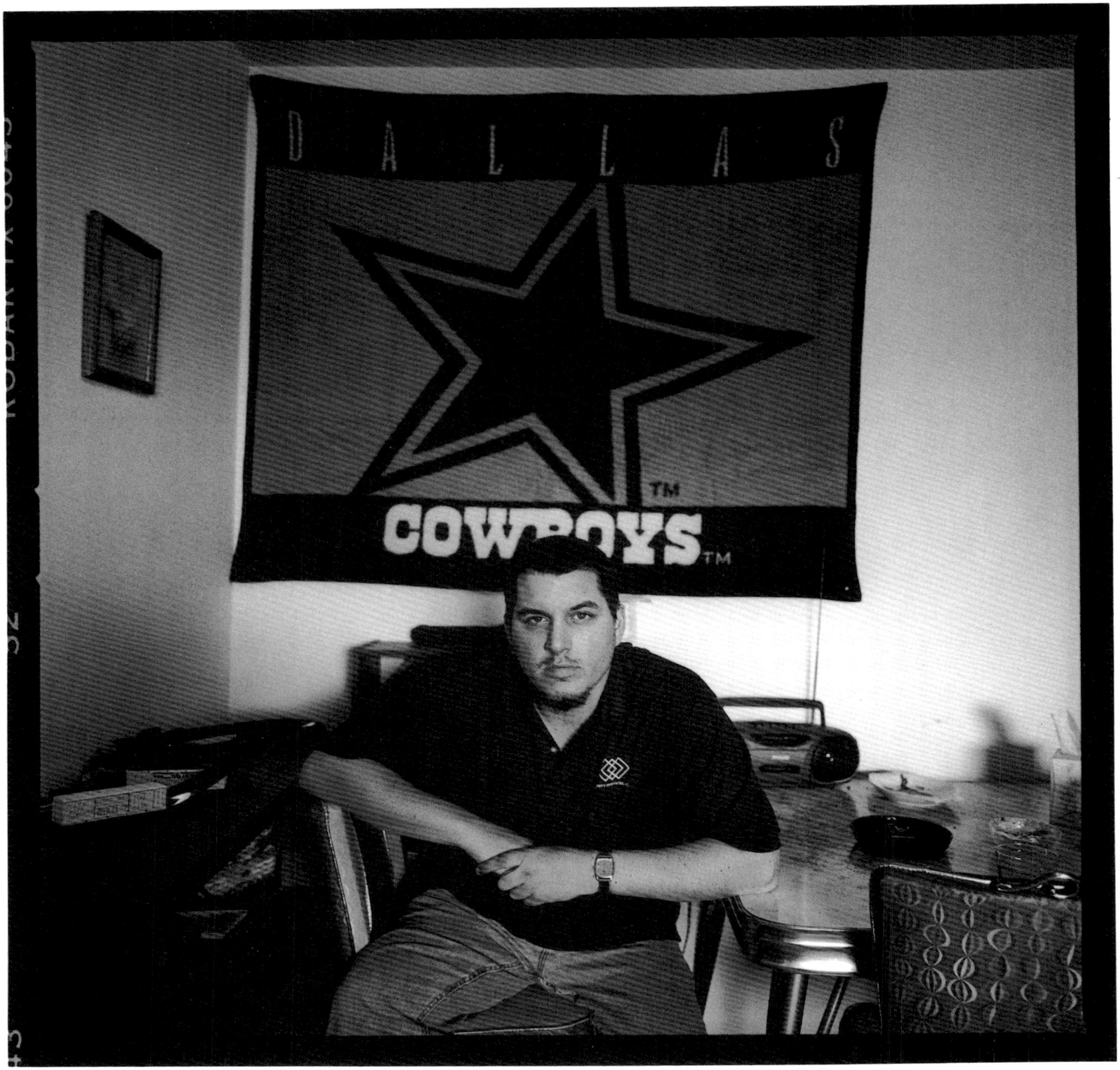
DALLAS
COWBOYS

Rich Spreitzer

Four years ago I was in the psychiatric ward at a local hospital. They discharged me and I came here.

Now I work in the recycling division at that same hospital. Me and some other guys grab all the papers from all the floors and bring them to the basement.

I can be nice or I can be mean. Sometimes I can even be comfortable holding on to other peoples' hands and starting things.

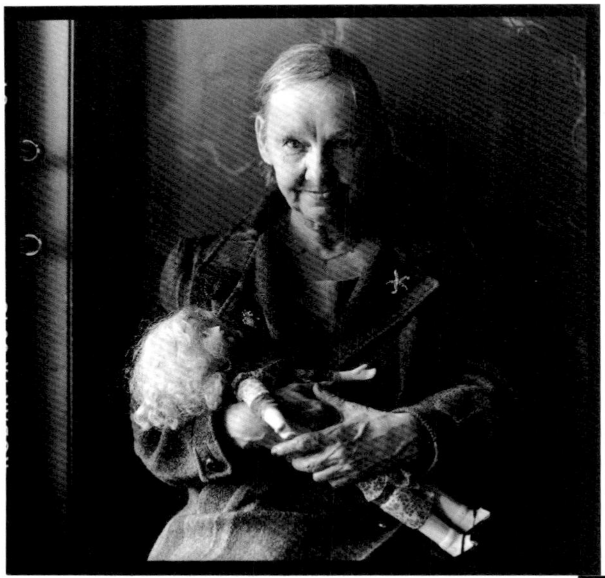

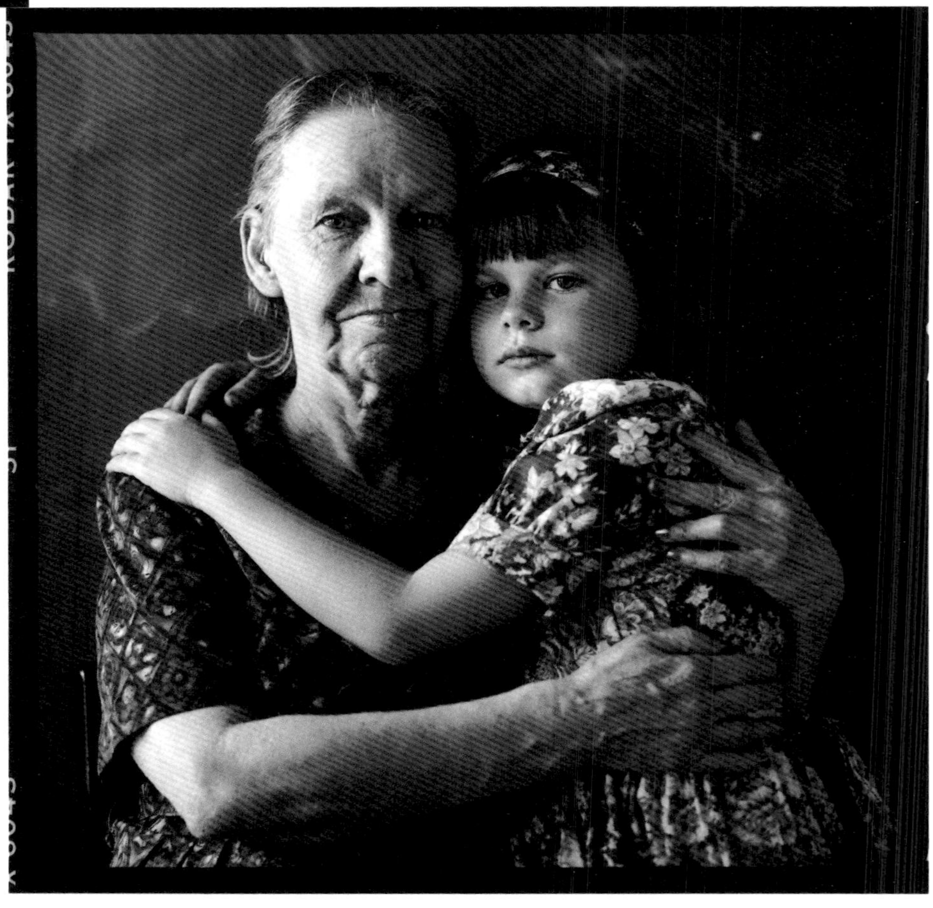

Irene

The image of an elderly woman holding a doll is reminiscent of institutional life for many mental health professionals. In secluded wards, some women pace halls for their entire lives while clinging to tattered dolls.

Irene spent most of her life in institutions, and when she came to the Lockport Center she brought a doll with her. She was encouraged to stop bringing it, as the doll was not healthy for her treatment and attracted curious stares as she walked down community streets.

A day treatment counselor heard that Irene was going to be photographed and suggested I bring a doll to the shooting to help Irene become comfortable as well as add a glow to her face. I planned on keeping the antique doll behind the camera, within Irene's sight. Irene, however, reached out for the doll — which she immediately named Doozie — and began cradling it.

Together, the doll and Irene serve as a haunting reminder of the past, a testament to the eerie behavior of institutional life. Yet Irene, who posed in the Roxy, had friends sitting all around her as the portrait was taken. They gave words of encouragement to her. They talked quietly about how happy and calm she looked. And, when the shutter clicked for the last time, Irene gave Marc a polite nod and walked away. She had other things to do that day.

In her second portrait, Irene interacts with Thane Dykstra's daughter, Kelsie, rather than an inanimate doll. Thirty years ago, Thane was passed around in the arms of patients at the Elgin State Mental Hospital. His father Art Dykstra was criticized for bringing his son to work with him. He was told a psychiatric ward was no place for an infant, that he'd be putting his son in danger. On the contrary, the young Thane brought vitality to the ward, if only for a few moments. Patients reached out to hold him, and smiled at the rare sight of an infant. Today, Thane's children regularly visit the Lockport Center and sometimes attend activities at the Roxy.

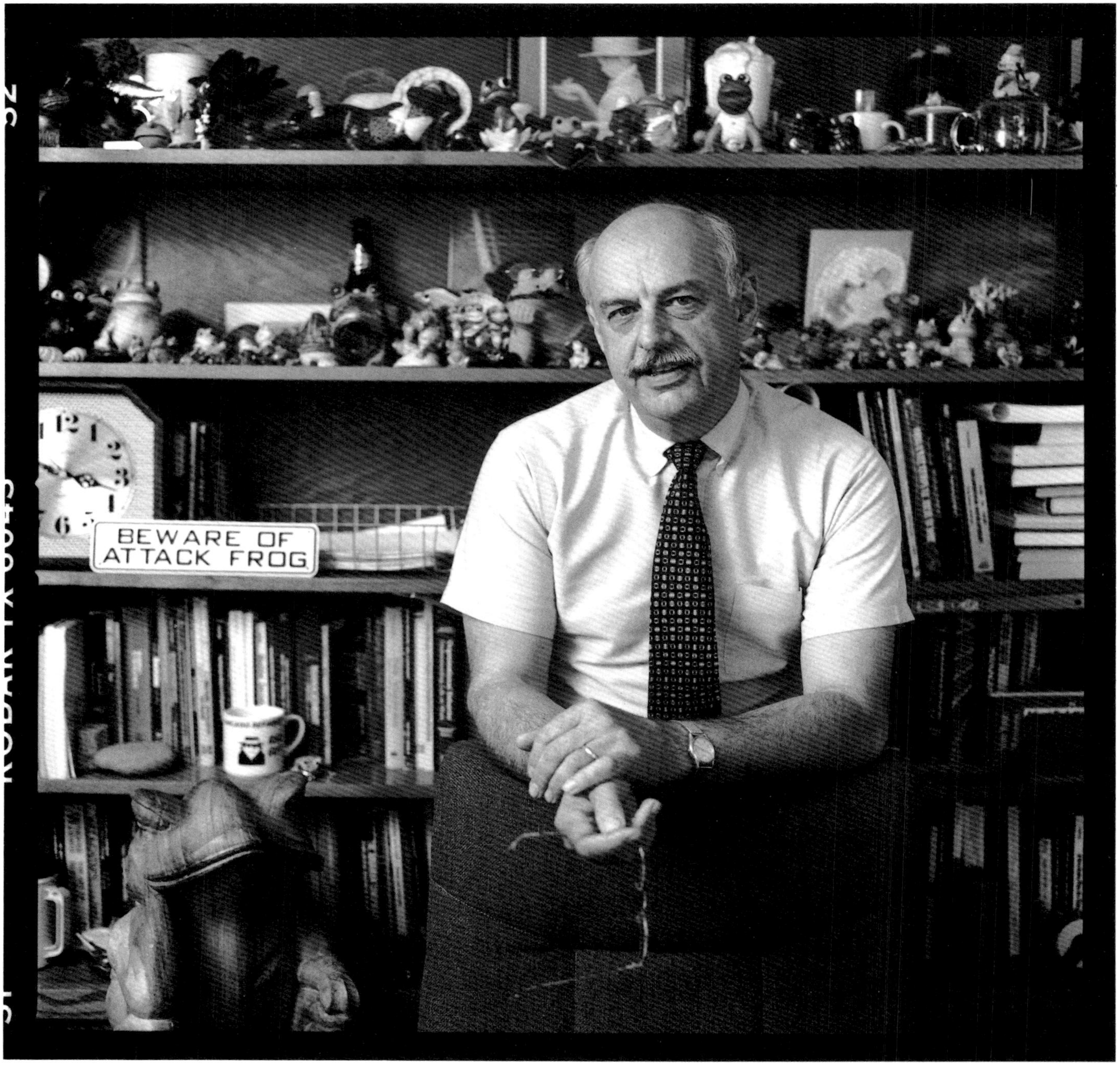
BEWARE OF
ATTACK FROG

Art Dykstra

I was in trouble with the system from the day I entered it. When I came to Elgin Mental Health Center in the mid 1960s there were many things I could not accept, from the sign that read *No Patients Allowed in the Treatment Rooms* to the fact that all the calendars in a 1,000-bed geriatric ward were from funeral homes. When I took those signs down I got a blue memo. A blue memo written about you meant that you did something wrong in the eyes of the administration. I got many blue memos.

What impressed me during this time was the number of people who worked in the mental health field who genuinely cared. I remember the incredible challenges and the staff members, whether educated or uneducated, who went beyond the call of duty to help the people we served. This is one reason I became an administrator. At that time the administration wasn't listening to the staff or the people we were trying to serve, and I decided I might be more effective as an administrator than a psychologist. I couldn't live with myself if I didn't try to change things.

Around this time I met Sharon Parker, who had people in her ward spending their entire lives without ever getting dressed. We tackled issues like abuse, the hydro-powered hoses used as punishment, and electric convulsive therapy. Looking back, the days at Elgin were challenging and good days because of all the changes going on.

One thing I think we do well at Trinity today is to offer people the opportunity to live in safe environments. I wouldn't want any person we serve and support living in a home I wouldn't live in myself. Today, I think the nation in general hasn't dealt with all the complexities of mental illness. The struggle I see is that there is no incentive to improve the spending patterns for people with mental illness or make higher-paying jobs available to the staff members. In terms of the treatment people receive, I feel like a lot of the day rooms I see today in hospitals and nursing homes are no different from the ones in the 1960s. They look like bus stations, with people just sitting around, not interacting. This is why I get so excited about the Roxy. It is a respectable and dignified way for people to hang out during the day and night. Why should anyone be condemned to a day room environment, always sitting, always waiting?

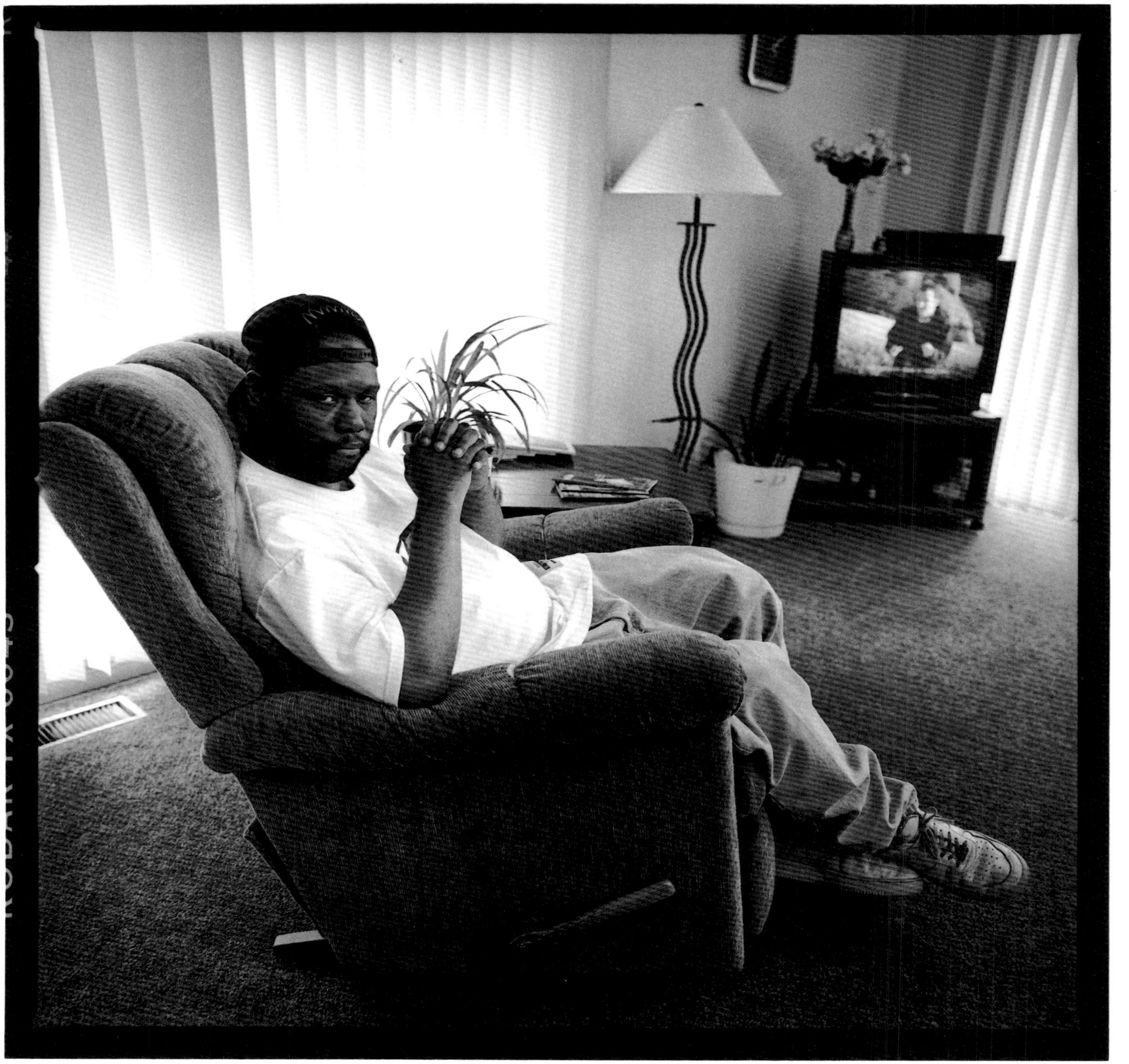

Darrell Smith

I'm a nice guy, unless someone messes with me. I mean like saying a mean comment or starting a fight. Now I will just go downstairs and chill or listen to music if this happens. I pretty much get along with all the guys in my house. I'm sitting in Brian's chair. He died in this house a few months ago. I don't think about him as much as I used to. But this is his chair and I won't forget it.

In the house I'm probably most close to Greg. I watch out for him when he gets seizures. I know how he's feeling, I used to get seizures.

Brian McGarry passed away January 10, 1998 after suffering a heart attack in the living room of his home in Joliet, Illinois. The thirty-seven-year-old man loved hanging out in the Roxy, and greeting both old and new friends with, "Hi, my name is Brian McGarry. I'm from Orland Park."

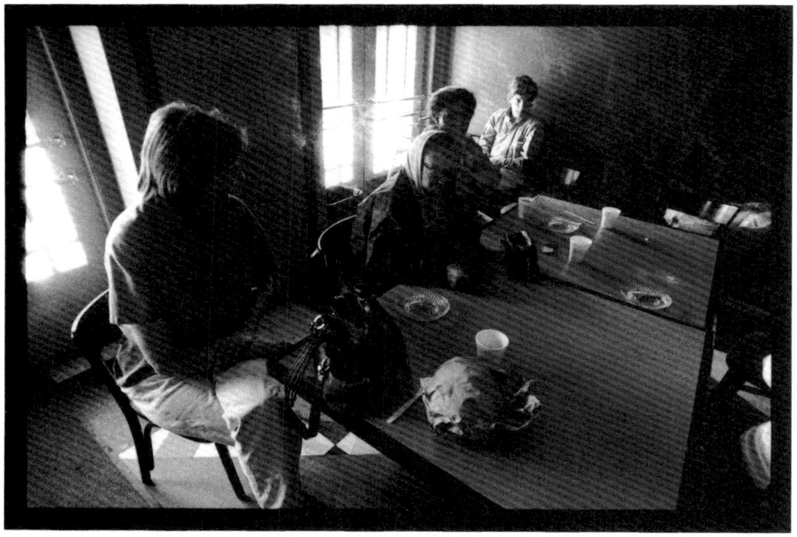

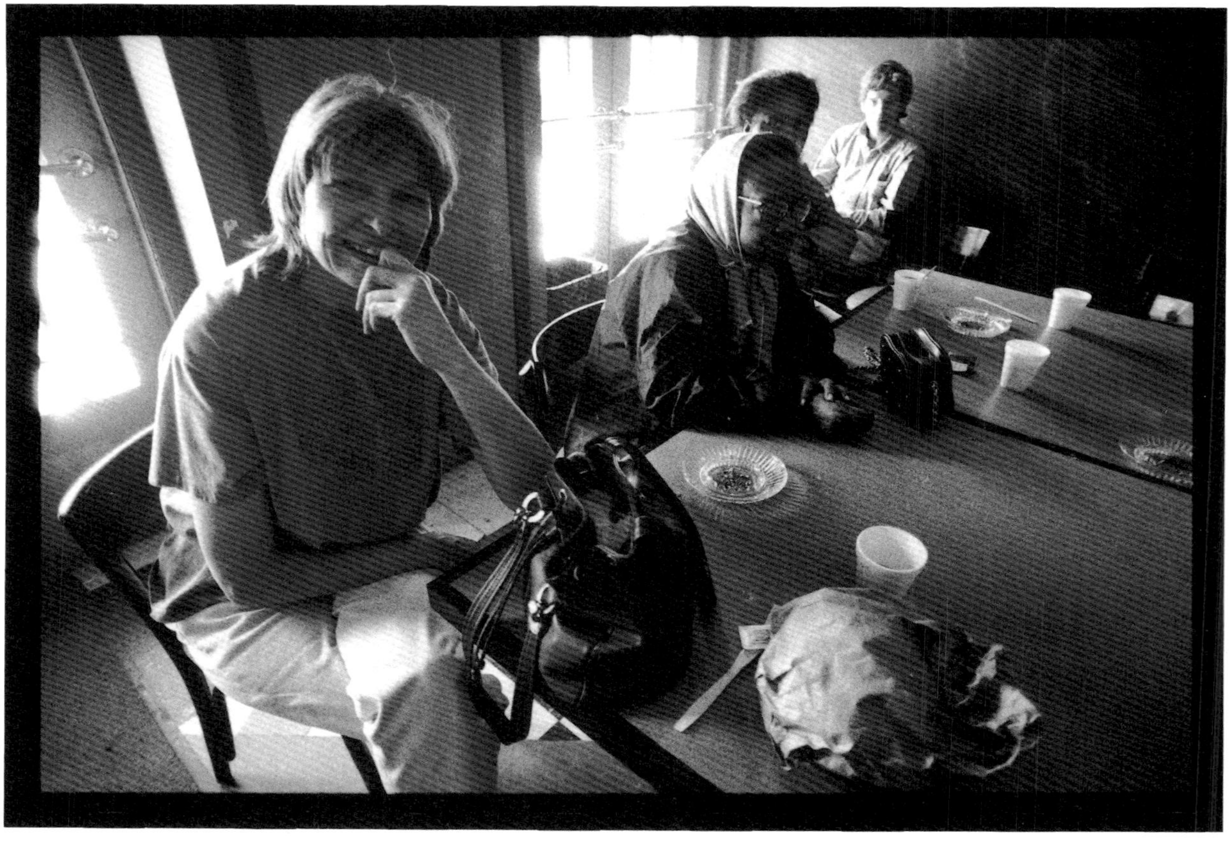

Carol Benson

When I first went into the hospital thirty years ago there was this other girl there who was trying to fill out the cards inside the magazines to get free copies. She asked me how to do it, so I showed her how to fill out her name and the other information. Then she started filling out all the cards from every magazine that was there. There were so many! I don't know why, but I said I'd help her. So I wrote her name down on all of them just so she wouldn't put down mine. My mother and I used to get magazines a long time ago, and we always paid for them.

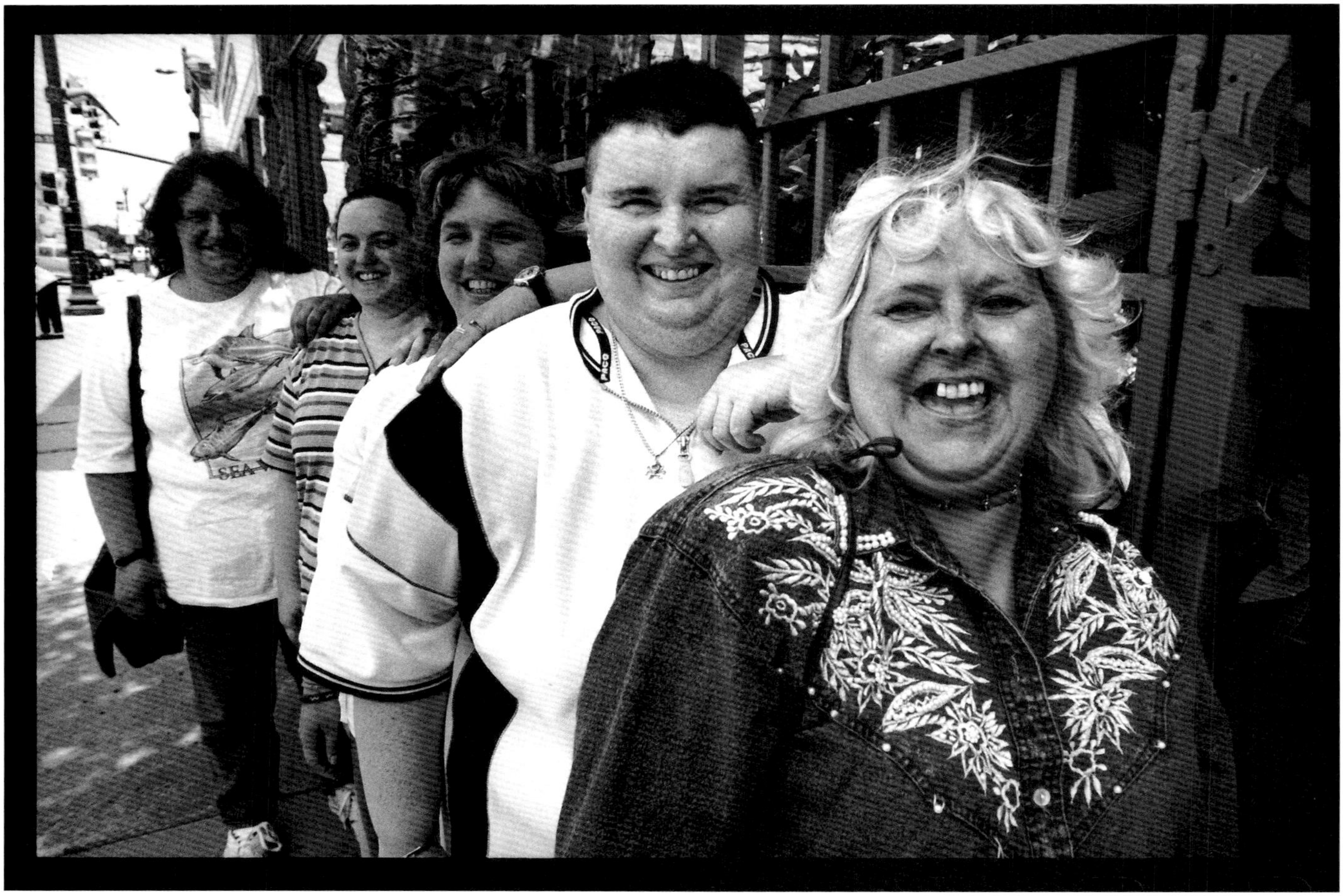
SEA

Cathy Ehmke

I've gotten to understand my illness. When I first came here my anger was really bad. I used to take twelve different types of meds, now I just take one.

When I was younger I was always alone. I was taught to be quiet and not say anything. I didn't know I was depressed until I came to Trinity — I didn't even know there was such a thing as an illness called depression. Basically, I'd been in and out of hospitals since I was twenty-three.

Here I have relationships with everyone. They support me when I'm down, help me socially and financially. I'm very happy now — I've got a lot of freedom, and I've really changed. I'm going for the goals of being with my kids, getting my driver's license, and getting my own place.

Pictured from right to left are: Cathy Ehmke, Kathy Molyneaux, Laura Chapman, Margaret Parsons, and Joanne Smith.

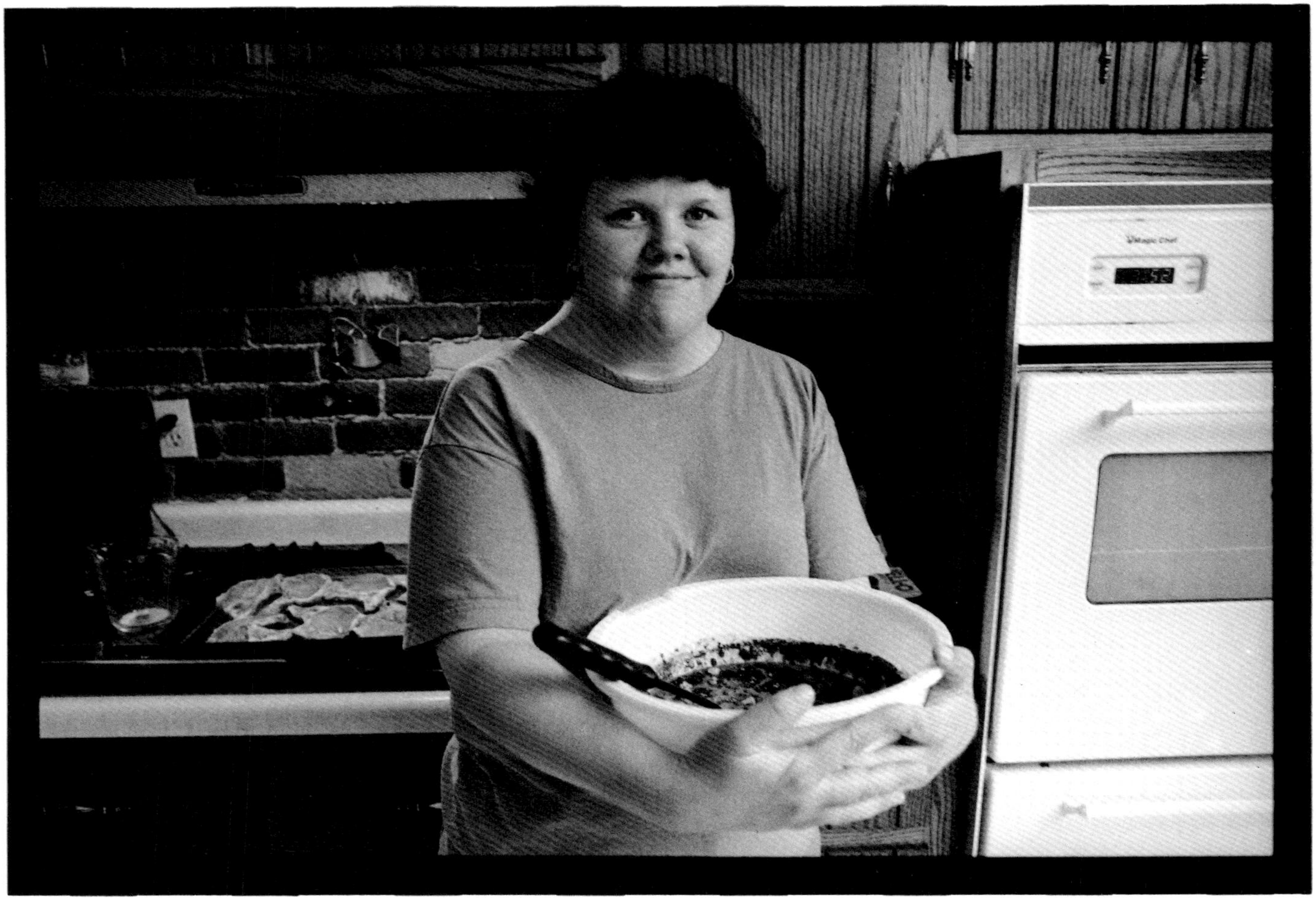

Pam Cole

I like to make chocolate pudding. The thing about pudding is that you can't eat too much of it or it'll make you fat and gain lots of pounds.

When I lived alone in Chicago, I used to cook for myself all the time. I'd cook pork chops, meatloaf, tacos, all kinds of stuff.

I like cooking, it's a nice experience. Even though one person in the house doesn't like my cooking, all the other ones do. That's fine with me.

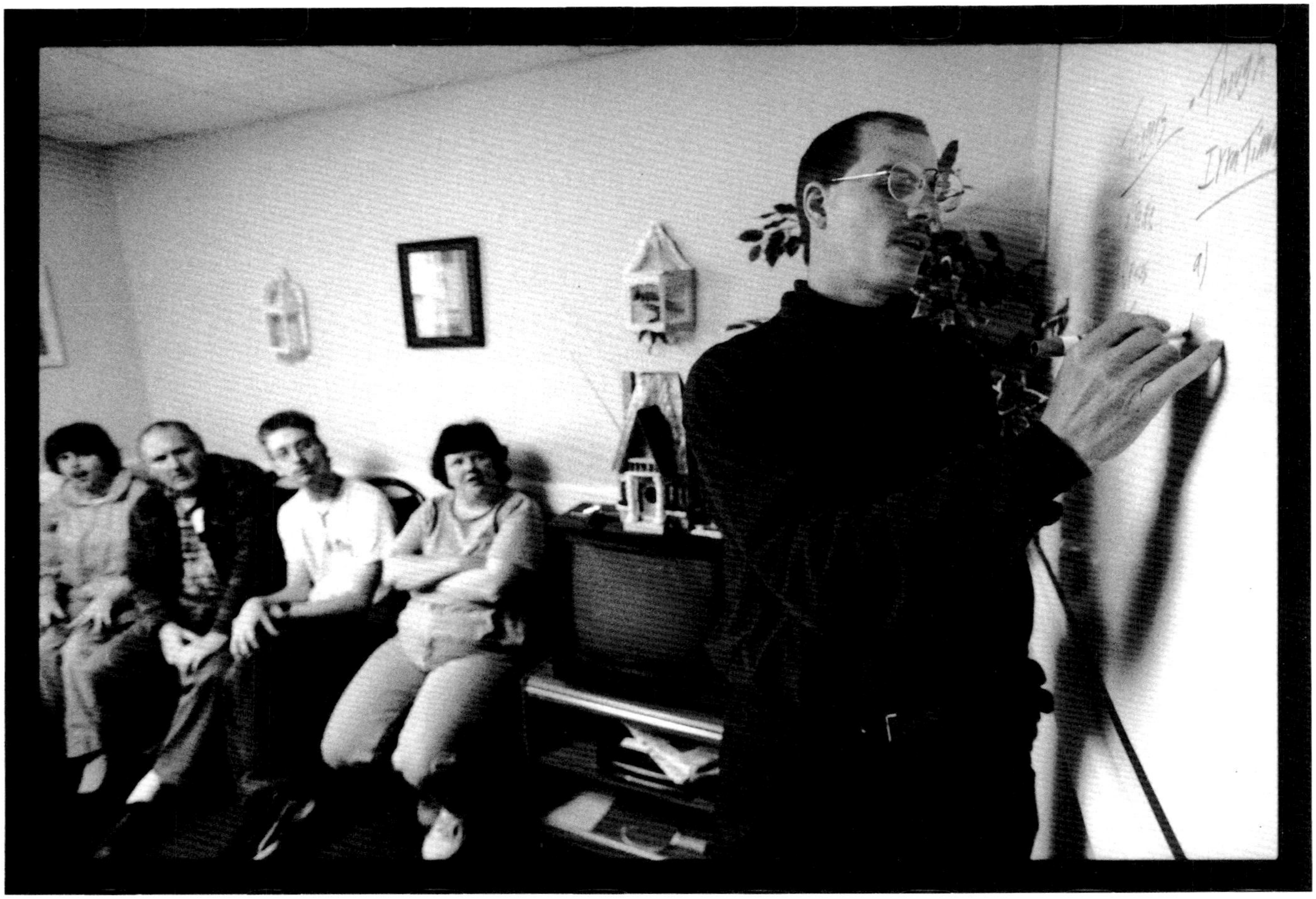

Behavior Chains with Thane Dykstra

"I'm ugly." "I have no friends." "Everything that happened was my fault." "I can't try that job again because I failed it last time." "The weather is bad so my whole day will be bad."

Welcome to the world of cognitive distortions, also known as cloudy thinking, negative thinking, or just plain stinkin' thinkin. In Behavior Chains, a weekly therapy group, participants work with Thane Dykstra on breaking down the process that leads to negative feelings, beginning with the powerful trigger. It can be sneaky like unanticipated foul weather, or expected like being called a hurtful name once again. This therapy is based in part on the work of David Burns in his book, Feeling Good.

On this particular morning, Thane asks the group to assist him in the creation of a behavior chain. And, drawing from real life, Thane selects the arrival of Marc and his assistant as a trigger. "What are some thoughts people have about getting their picture taken?" he asks. "I'm ugly," someone says. Another adds, "I look bad in pictures."

Thane then encourages the participants to cite the accompanying feelings that result from these thoughts, like fearfulness and nervousness. The next step involves citing evidence to back up the original thought. Answers vary from, "I always look bad in pictures," to, "Cameras upset me." Usually, most of the evidence can be attributed to one of the types of cognitive distortions, like over-generalization or black-and-white thinking. The following examples were discussed by the group:

Over-generalization: "I looked bad in the last few pictures of myself, so I'll always look ugly."

Black-and-white thinking: "If I get my picture taken here everyone will associate me with being mentally ill."

Fortune-telling: "I just know I'll look ugly when the picture comes out."

Mind-reading: "Marc probably doesn't like my hair. I don't think he'll even want me in these pictures. I'm not good enough."

Personalization: "Why do they want to take a picture of me? I'm not special."

After recognizing that your thoughts are sometimes fueled by negative distortions, it's important to think of rational responses, Thane notes. The group proceeds to discuss alternative responses and ways to prevent cognitive distortions from dictating how they will live and feel.

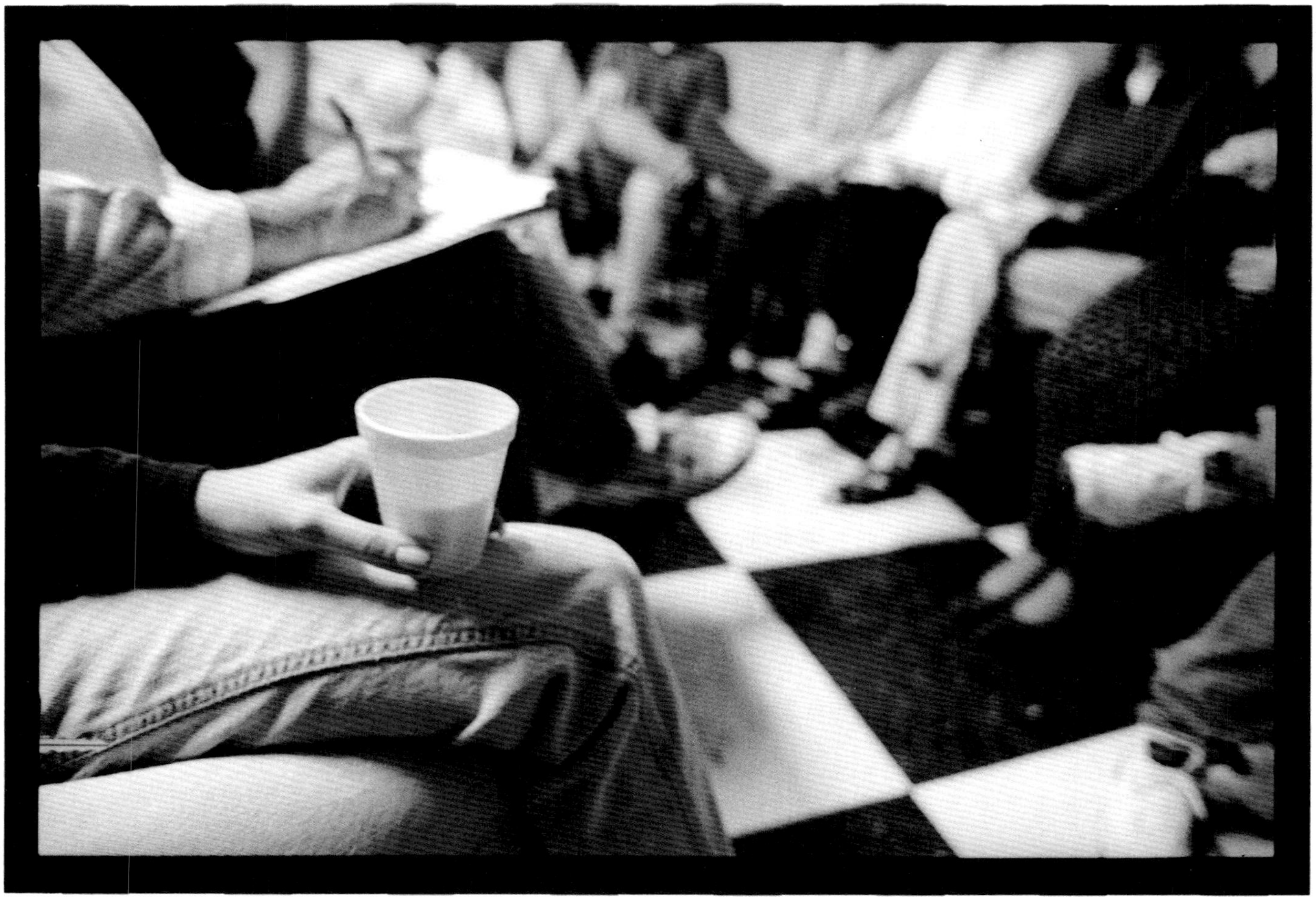

The Staff

Every Monday afternoon, the therapists, counselors, nurses, and team leaders meet to discuss clinical issues in the Roxy basement. Meeting times range from a half-hour to over two hours. There are plenty of notepads, daily planners, and an occasional cup of coffee.

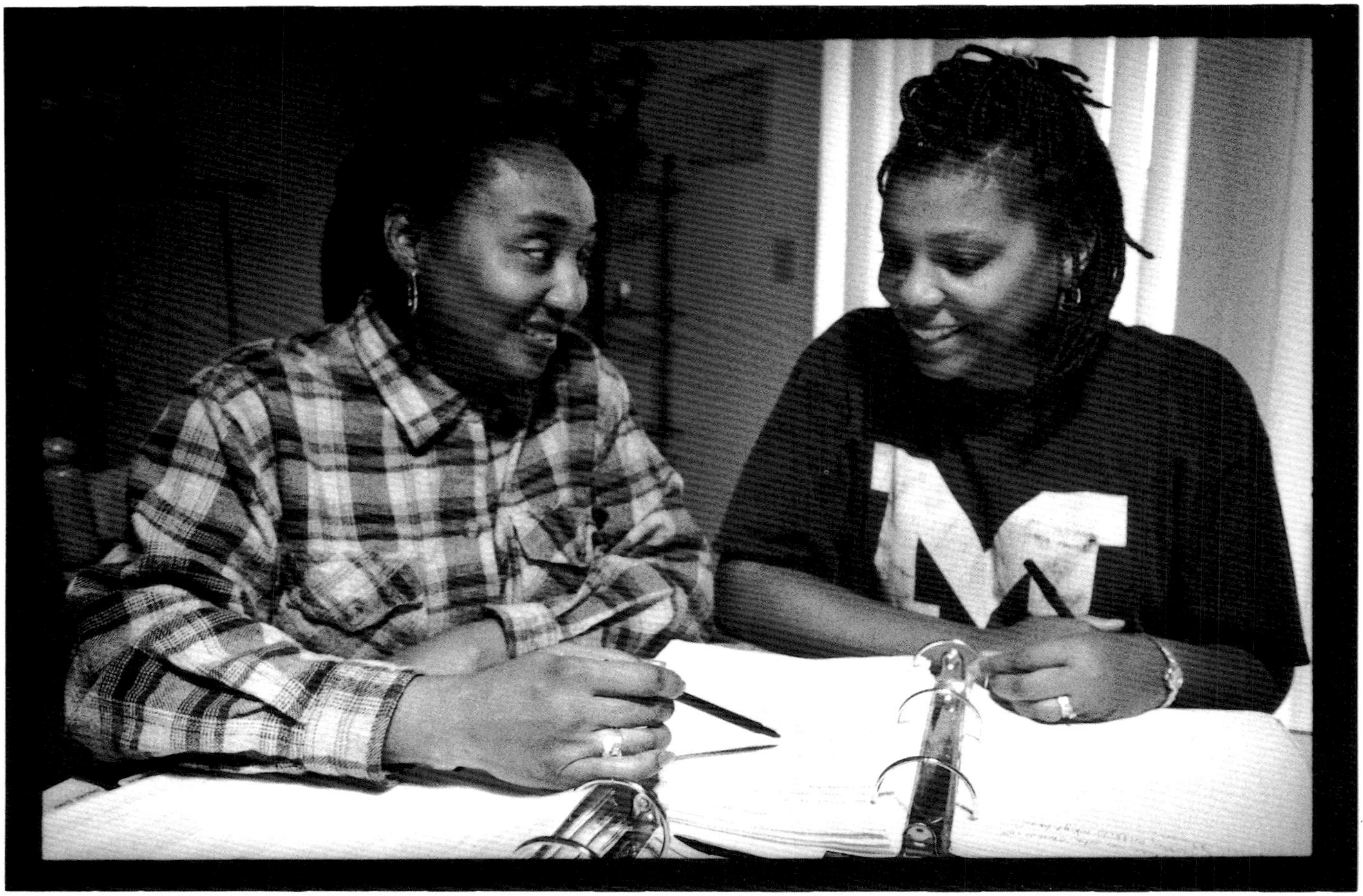

Marquetia Smith & Betty Woods

Marquetia and Betty are independent living counselors. They work the 3:00–11:00 p.m. evening shift at a house in Lockport where six women live, including Pam Cole, Sue Fencl, and Colli Koger. Marquetia and Betty are responsible for transporting the women, assisting them with cooking and cleaning, and counseling the women as needed.

Marquetia: Every time we come in we read the communication sheet to find out how the previous shift went, and what to expect from the ladies. I would describe my job as challenging, because that's exactly what it is. Understanding mental illness requires a lot of patience. I think it takes a special type of person to work this particular job. I've been here almost three years.

If I lived in a neighborhood where there was a group home, I might expect that home to be the worst. You don't know anything about them except that they have some problems. We treat this house the way we would want others to treat our homes. We help the ladies understand how a house should be, how it should look, and how they should act. Because the majority of our neighbors are expecting the worst.

What I enjoy most about my job is the personalities of all the women in this house. They've taught me that they are no different than myself. Their mental illness might mean that they may not be able to cope as well as others or deal with certain situations. That's about the only difference.

Betty: When you think about a person who's mentally ill, you think "crazy, totally out of it." Or at least that's what the stereotypes are. I know from working here that the truth is these women have feelings and unique personalities. I think it's very helpful and beneficial that this house is in a community. The people we serve can see how people without disabilities live and be among them rather than set apart.

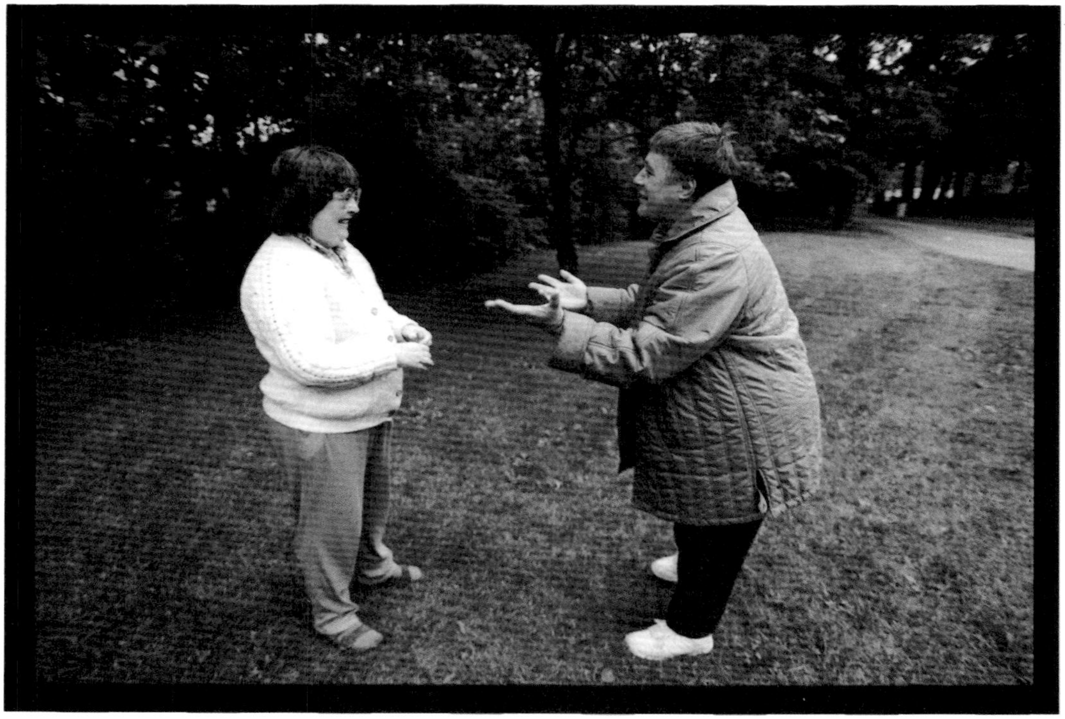

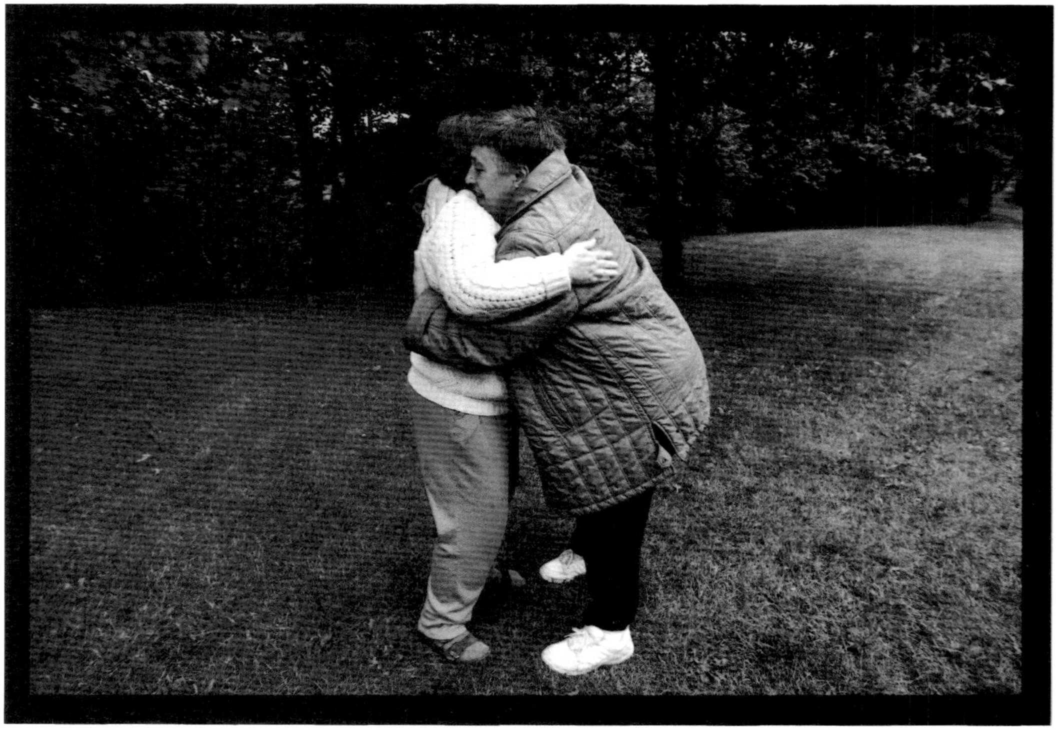

Role-Playing for Real Life

How do you "act" while you're waiting for a bus? Do you make eye contact with the person standing across from you in an elevator? What happens if a cashier fails to give you the proper amount of change? Do you file a complaint or walk away with your shoulders hunched?

In the Social Skills group, people work on role-playing various life situations and practicing appropriate body language and responses. They learn that all the world really is a stage, and people do scrutinize behavior and find fault with patterns that are disruptive or abnormal.

"We take on the roles that people play in the community, like standing in line at the movies or the bus stop. We create real life situations and act out responses to them," said John Frost, a co-facilitator and day treatment counselor.

Sheryl Caudle and Shirley Jadczak pause for a moment before beginning their acting scene. They have been instructed to pretend they are sisters who have not seen each other for a long time.

"You're stepping off the train, you see her coming," a counselor says. "Lots of emotion! Great!"

They embrace beneath the trees. They continue looking each other up and down in joy.

"Has she changed her haircut?," she continues. "Look at each other at arm's length. Great!"

Sheryl and Shirley continue their scene as the rest of the actors look on. In a few moments they, too, will enter the grassy stage and perform a short scene.

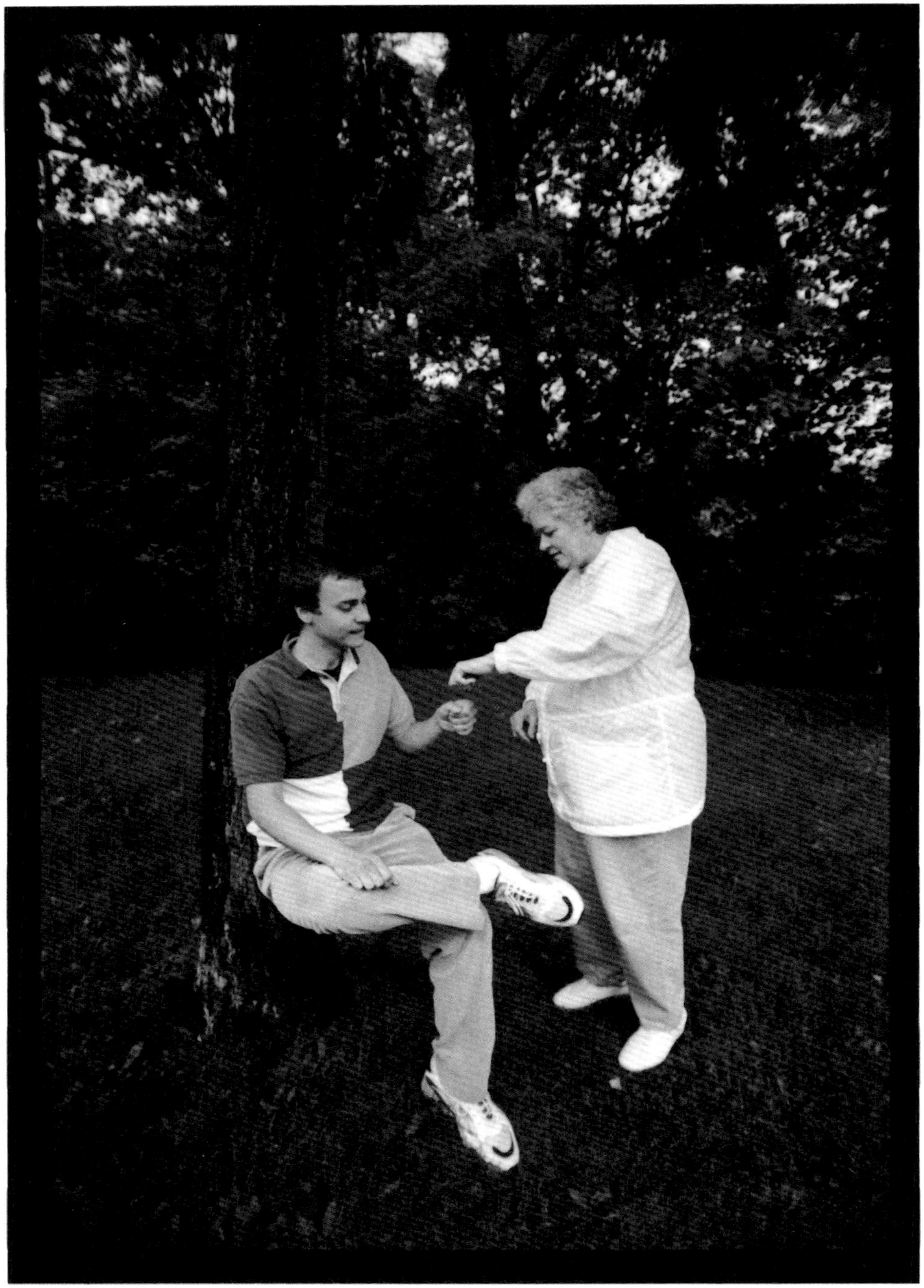

Role-Playing on the Job

Jane Stuckey pours coffee for Jon Frost while portraying a waitress. For two months in 1959, Jane worked as a waitress, but had to quit because the restaurant was too far away from her home. Here she hones her serving skills so the group can guess what type of situation she and Jon are acting out.

"Cream and sugar?" she asks.

The group often plays employee and customer roles to prepare themselves for community interactions.

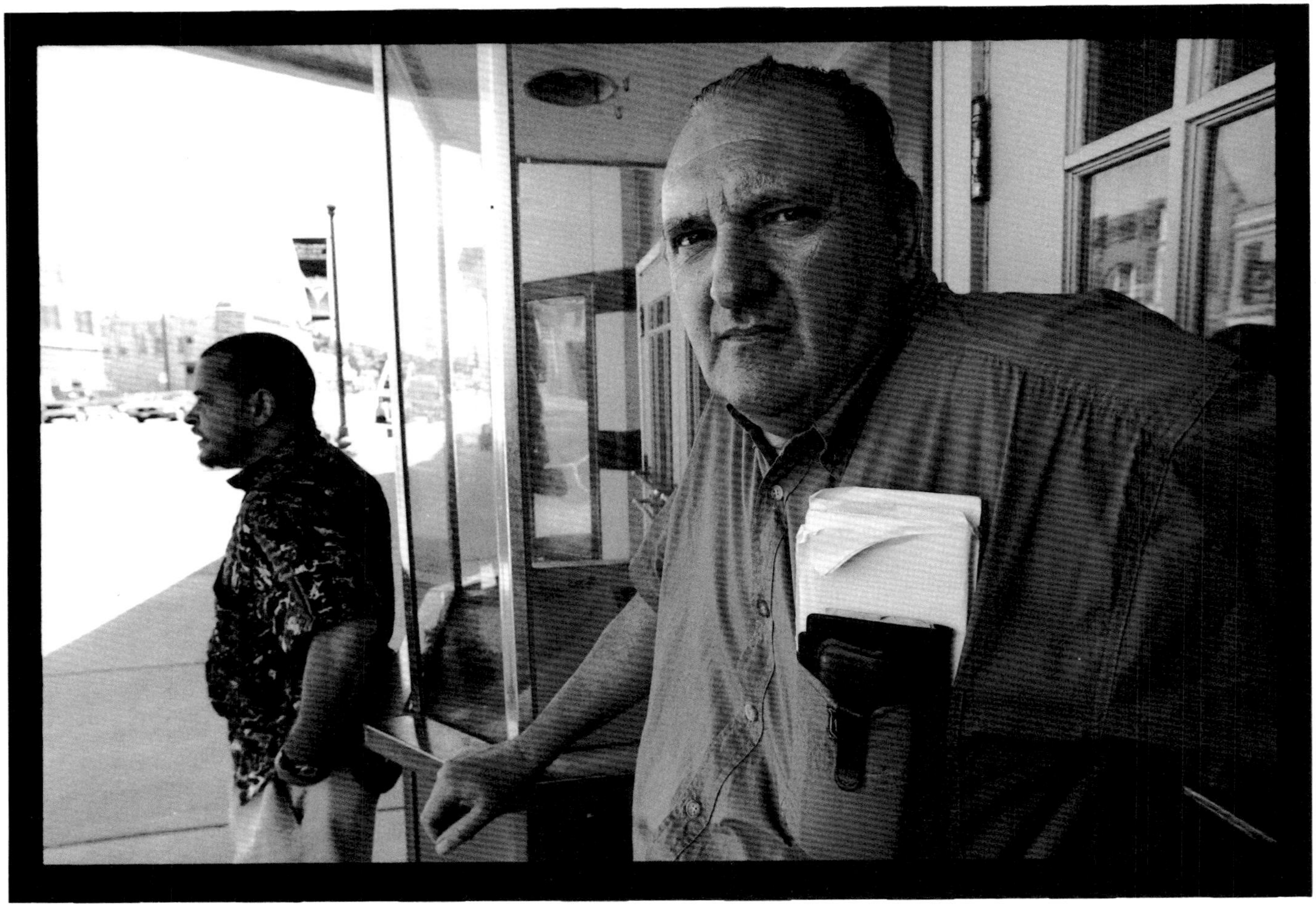

Dave Harding

I have my ups and downs.
I jump around like a Mexican jumping bean —
but I'm resilient.
I come back to my regular self.

Dave made the above statement after I asked him to describe his overall personality. He didn't intend it to be a poem, but I broke the lines down and sort of created one. Dave works as a custodian for the Roxy, and shares an apartment with Tony Rivera.

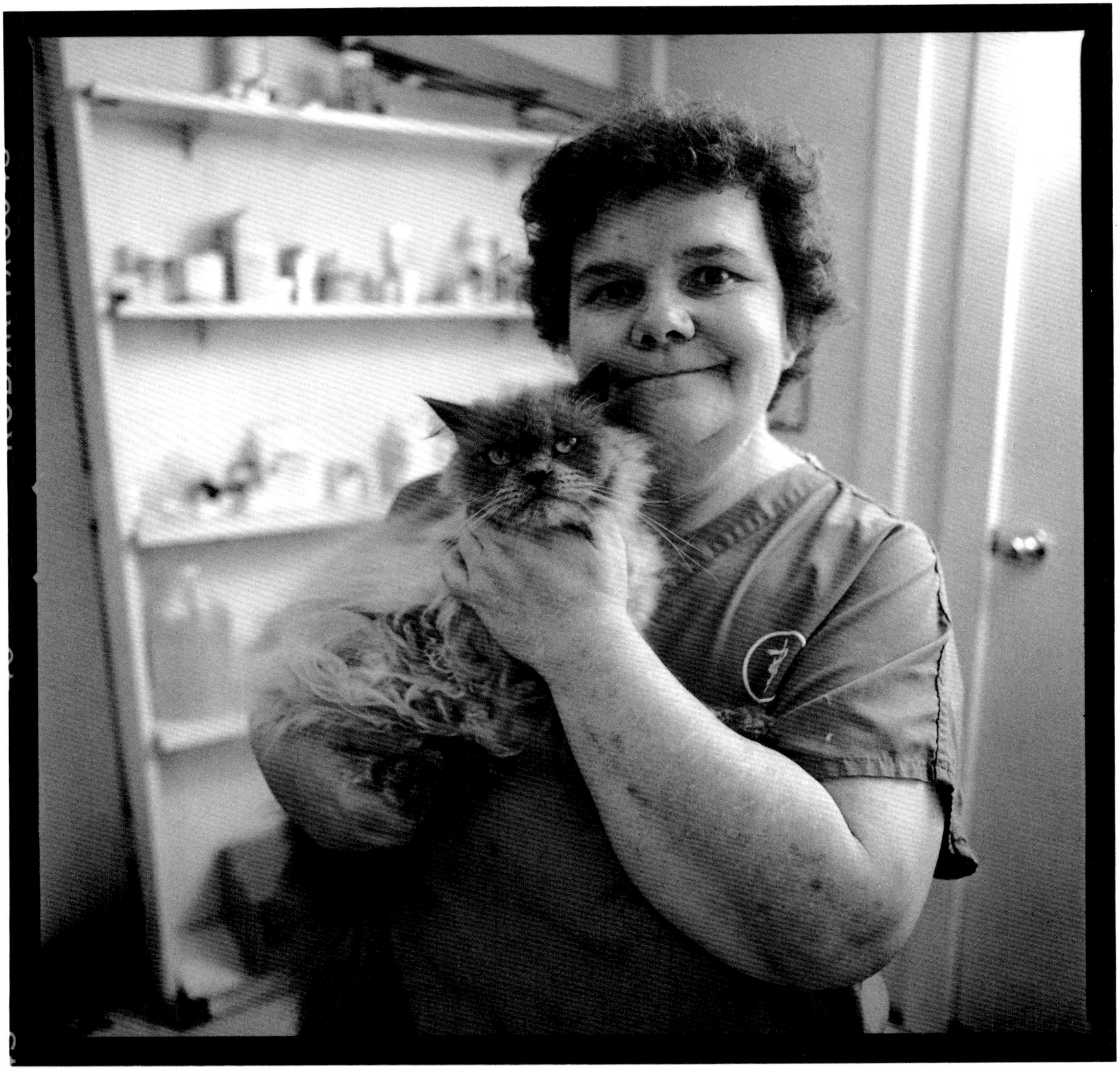

Rose Clark

I'm a refrigerator magnet collector, crochet instructor, student, bowler, shoulder to cry on, and friend to laugh with. Sometimes I wake up so sick, but then I go to work and feel better. Being with the animals, it makes me feel a hundred percent better. Does that sound funny?

I love my boss. He's crazy. When he does surgery he dances, does the jitterbug. Sometimes I go into surgery with him to make sure all the animals are lying down straight and not awake. Mostly my responsibilities are taking care of the cages and general cleaning.

I've been with Trinity four years. Since then I've gone back into school, gotten a job with cleaning the Lockport Center and now here in the community, live in my own apartment, got two cats, and have a checking and a savings account.

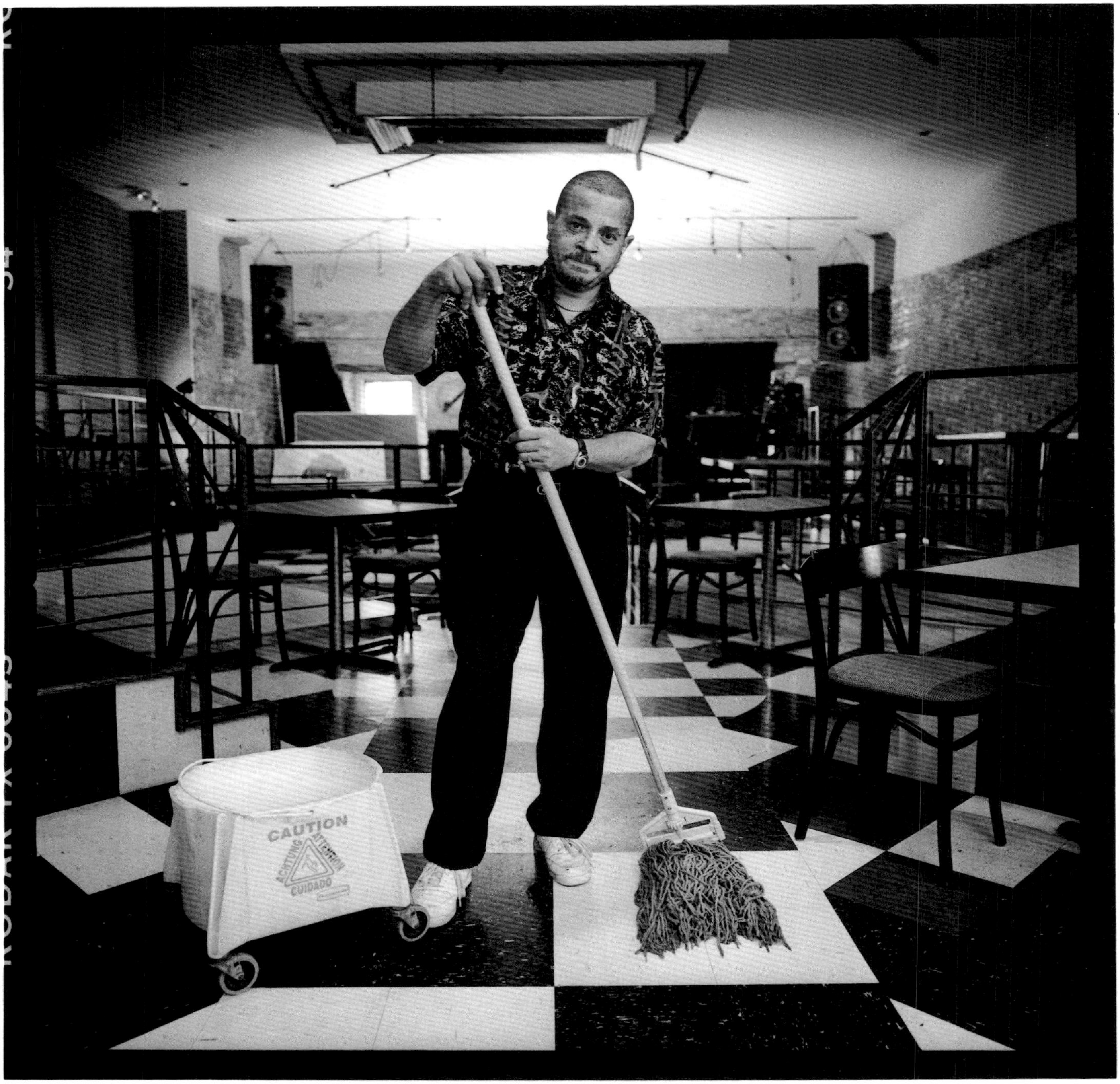
CAUTION
ACHTUNG
ATTENTION
CUIDADO

Wayne Wilson

The best way to mop is with a damp, not soapy, mop. I've worked this job almost ten months. It's pretty easy. The job coaches don't hassle you while you're working.

I used to be a draftsman for an electrical company, and I worked in an office. We were drafting electric conveyor ducts. You had to be very, very precise. I worked there for one year and eight months. I got laid off because me and this other guy smoked marijuana on the job. This was all happening in 1975. I stopped doing drugs and haven't smoked marijuana since 1977.

Some people think that because you have a mental illness you can't do nothing. They say you're violent, so you can't work. Or you're dumb, so you can't learn anything. Right now my goal is to keep working and move from a group home into an apartment. My therapist Keith says, "If it's not broke, don't try and fix it." It's the best advice I've gotten in a while.

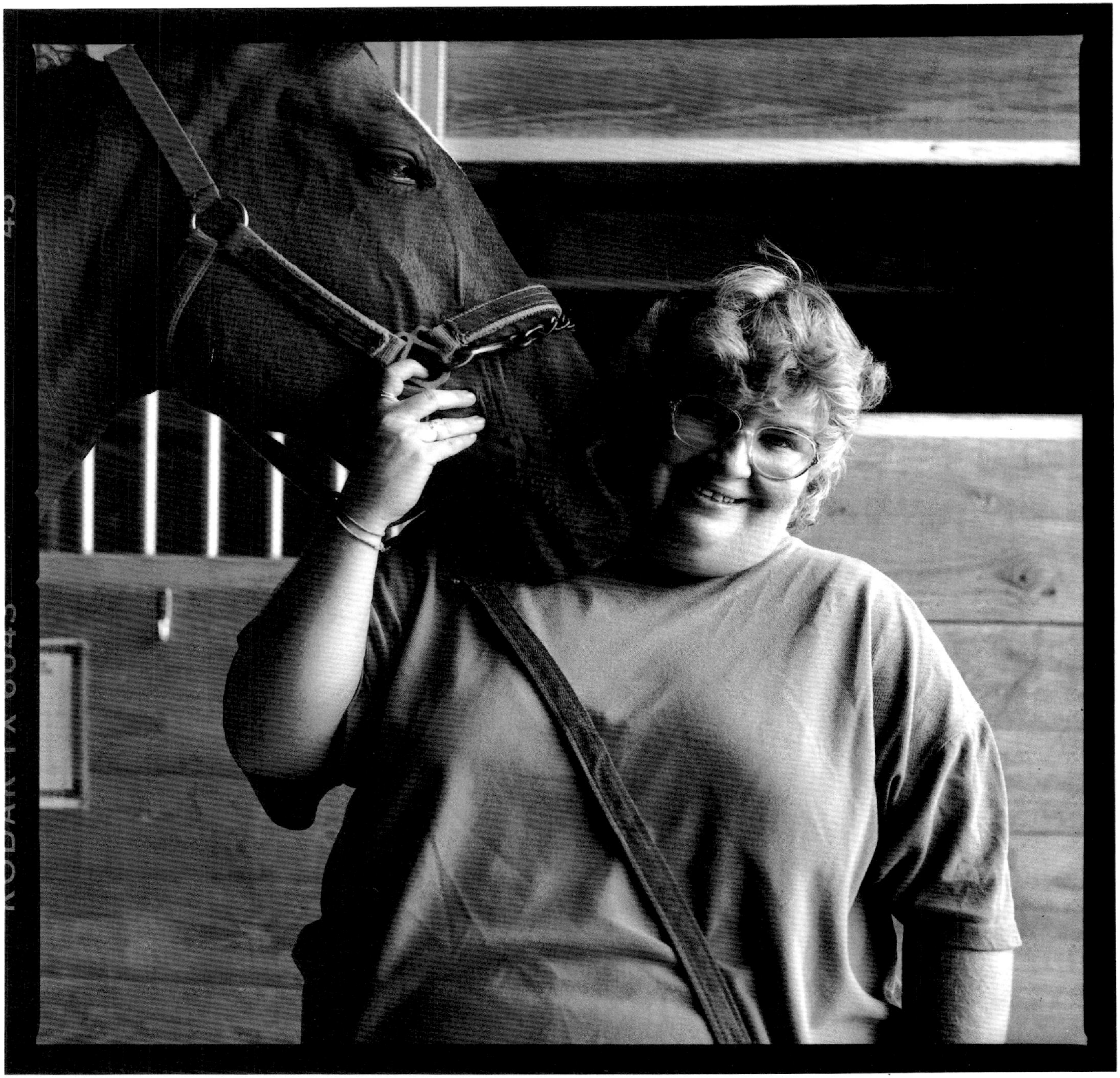

Siobhan Brennan

I think Wolf just wants to run free and go very far. One day I'd like to own a farm and let him run and run. Every time I give him a carrot he'll rest his head on my shoulder and use it to scratch his itches. I don't mind it. I'm used to it.

Before I got a job at Strides I was working in a fast food restaurant. I like working with the animals. Each of us has a horse that we have to take care of while we're here. I lead Wolf around while people ride him and also clean his stall. I've been working here for two years.

Mostly I like walking with Wolf when nobody else is around. When we are alone I feel very calm.

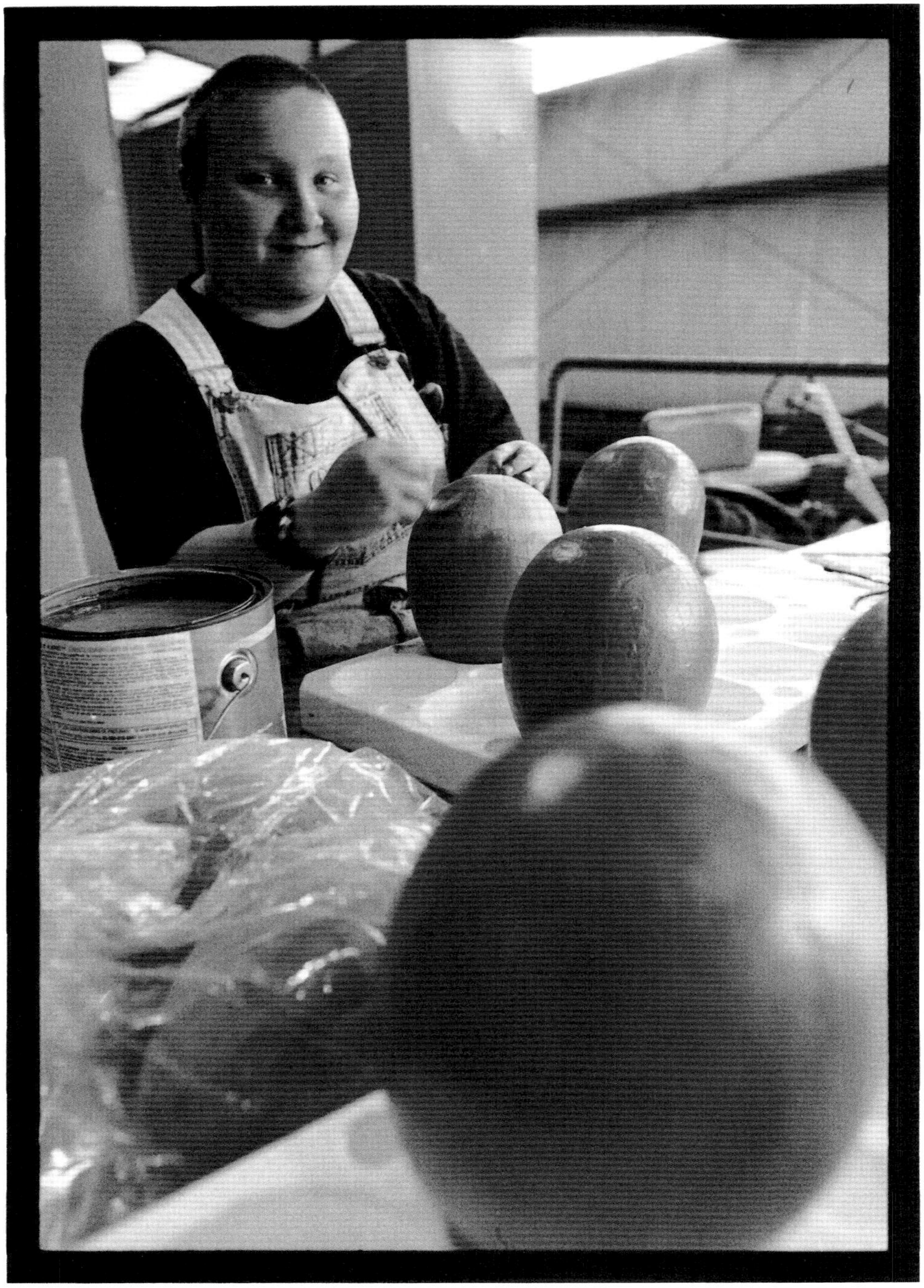

Barb Centkowski

So, Barb, what's with that weird thing you're painting orange?

Hey, this weird orange thing is going to turn into my paycheck! Don't knock it. No, seriously, we call them eggheads. They use them for making different crafts at Petals & Twigs [Trinity's gift shop]. This one will probably turn into something for Halloween. I've been doing this job for two years. I like it, it's something different that I've never done before. We paint all kinds of things.

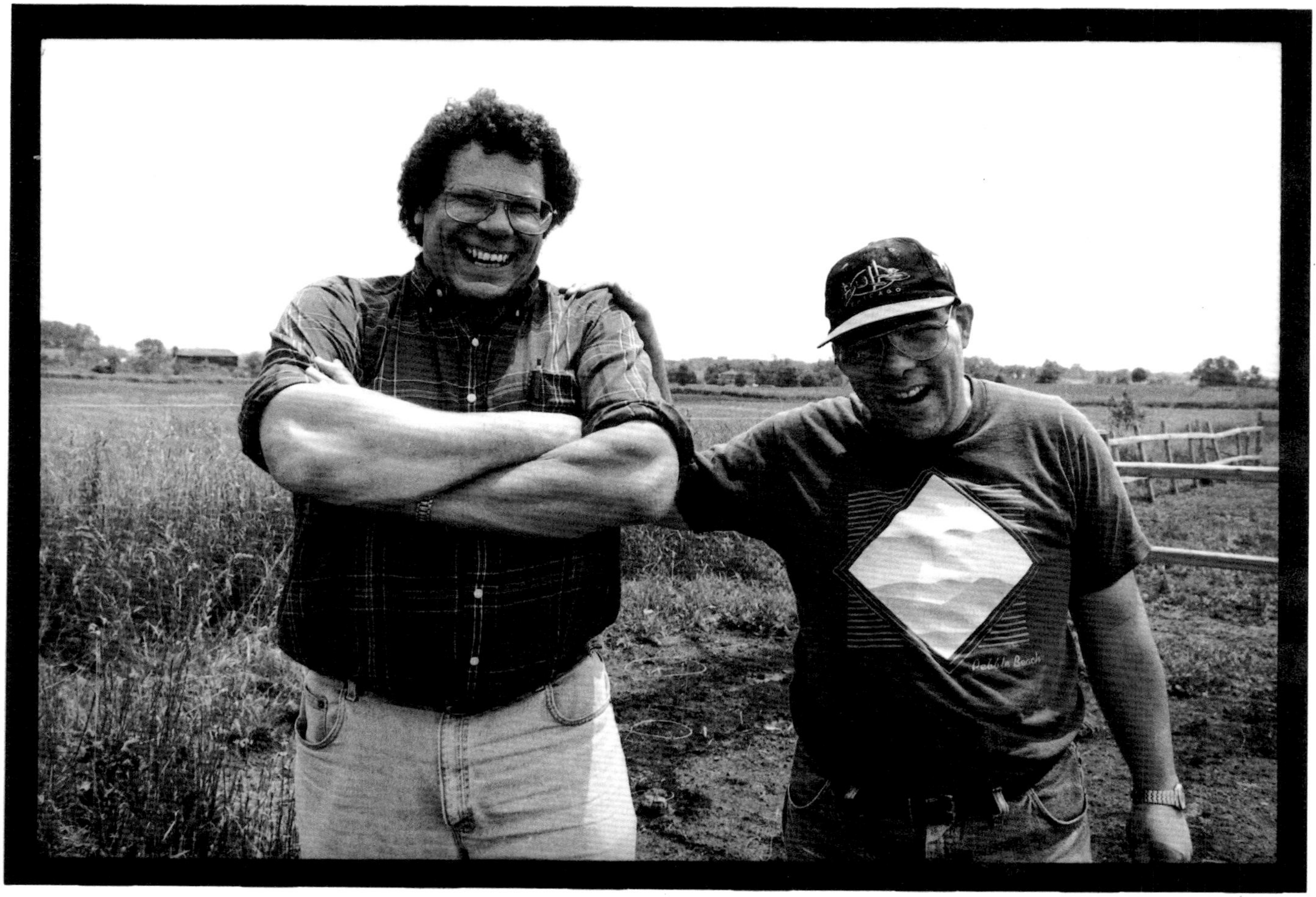

Bill Kahoun

We looked at stores, offices, supermarkets, and even considered opening our day treatment site in a rural farmhouse nearby. I personally think that the key word in psycho-social is "social" and didn't see the point of having our site in a rural area. When we looked at the bank building in the middle of a downtown area, we were excited. We were up front with the city of Lockport about who we were, and they were very receptive to us.

Our main concern from the get-go was the impression we were going to make on the actual city. We've had a few tough times, but, overall, I'm pleased with our progress.

Soon after we opened, we contacted Strides and started bringing some people there. It's been beneficial for guys like Paul, who are hard to get to go to groups and sometimes get uncooperative. Paul comes to Strides very reliably, and he'll come no matter what mood or frame of mind he's in. To me, this indicates that there's something there for this guy, whether it's touching the horses, or the environment, or the experience of learning ways to make the horse do things, or even working in the garden.

One time in particular, we had a person who went to Strides a lot and was going through a tough time in his life. He was going to be participating in a horse show, but a day or two before the show his doctor wanted to put him in the hospital. He told his doctor he wanted to participate in the show. He ended up placing and winning an award. I think there's just something about being around a horse that makes people want to persevere and succeed.

Bill Kahoun is the day treatment program director. In this photograph, he's hanging out in the Strides garden with Paul Miller.

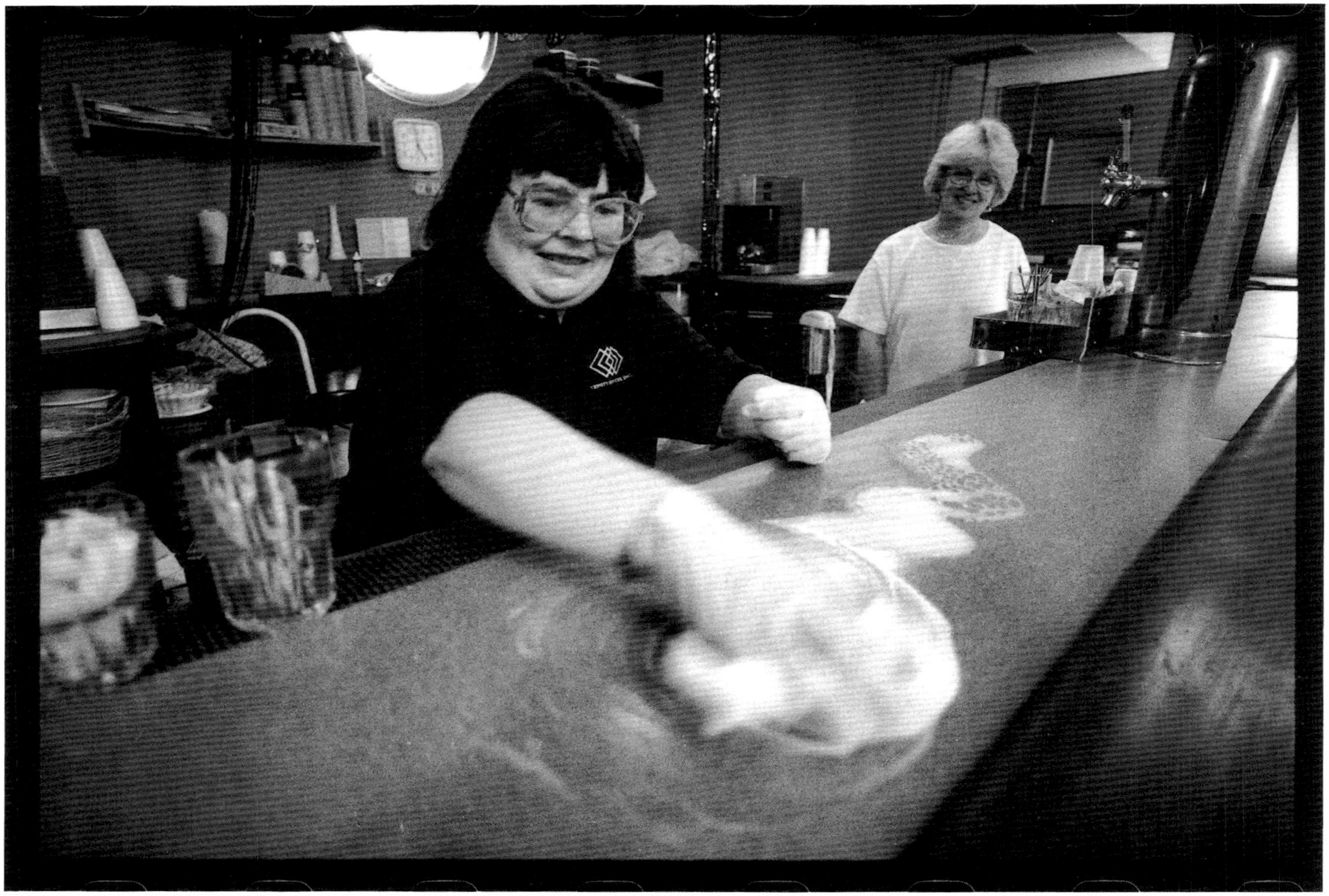

Sheryl Caudle

My family at first didn't understand why I was so depressed. My dad kept asking me why couldn't I be happy? Well, I couldn't be happy right then.

I never thought I'd be able to work again, because of my illness. Other jobs in the past I've had to quit, but I don't want to quit cleaning the Roxy. At first I felt like quitting, because I was feeling a little bit like I did in the past, when I handled vending machine routes in Dekalb, Illinois. I was starting to stress out a little bit. But then I remembered that I want to have an apartment someday, and a job in the community. Both of these things would be special to me if I had them, because it would mean I've come a long way.

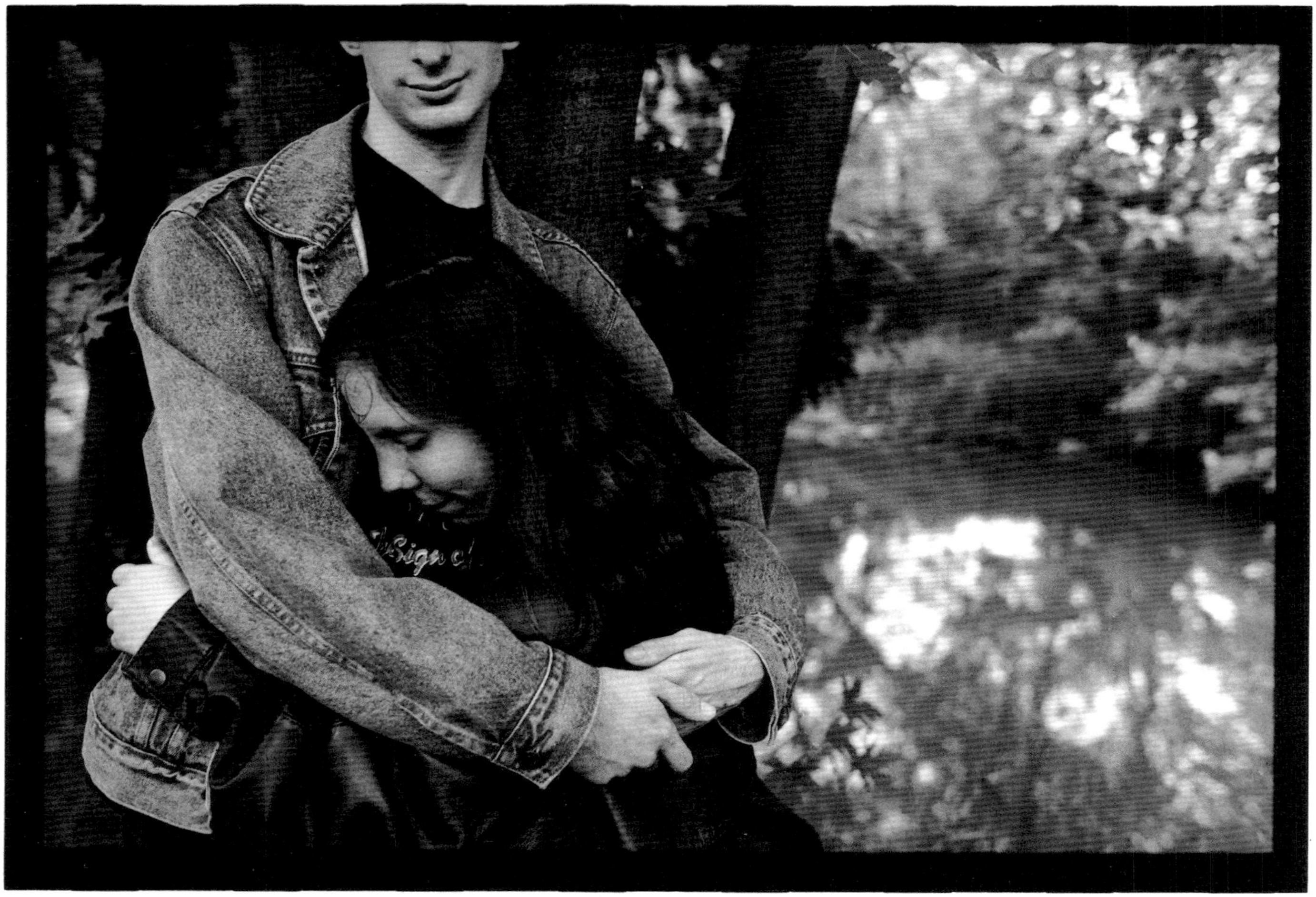

Colli Koger

We met last year when Jim was visiting the program to see if he liked it. I was already here. I don't remember how we started dating. We talk and laugh and giggle. He says he loves me and that I'm sexy. It makes me happy.

There's a hole in my heart, and I've had three surgeries — in 1984, 1986, and 1987. I work at the Roxy two nights a week and clean. I'm trying to save money to go to Disneyland with Jim and his family.

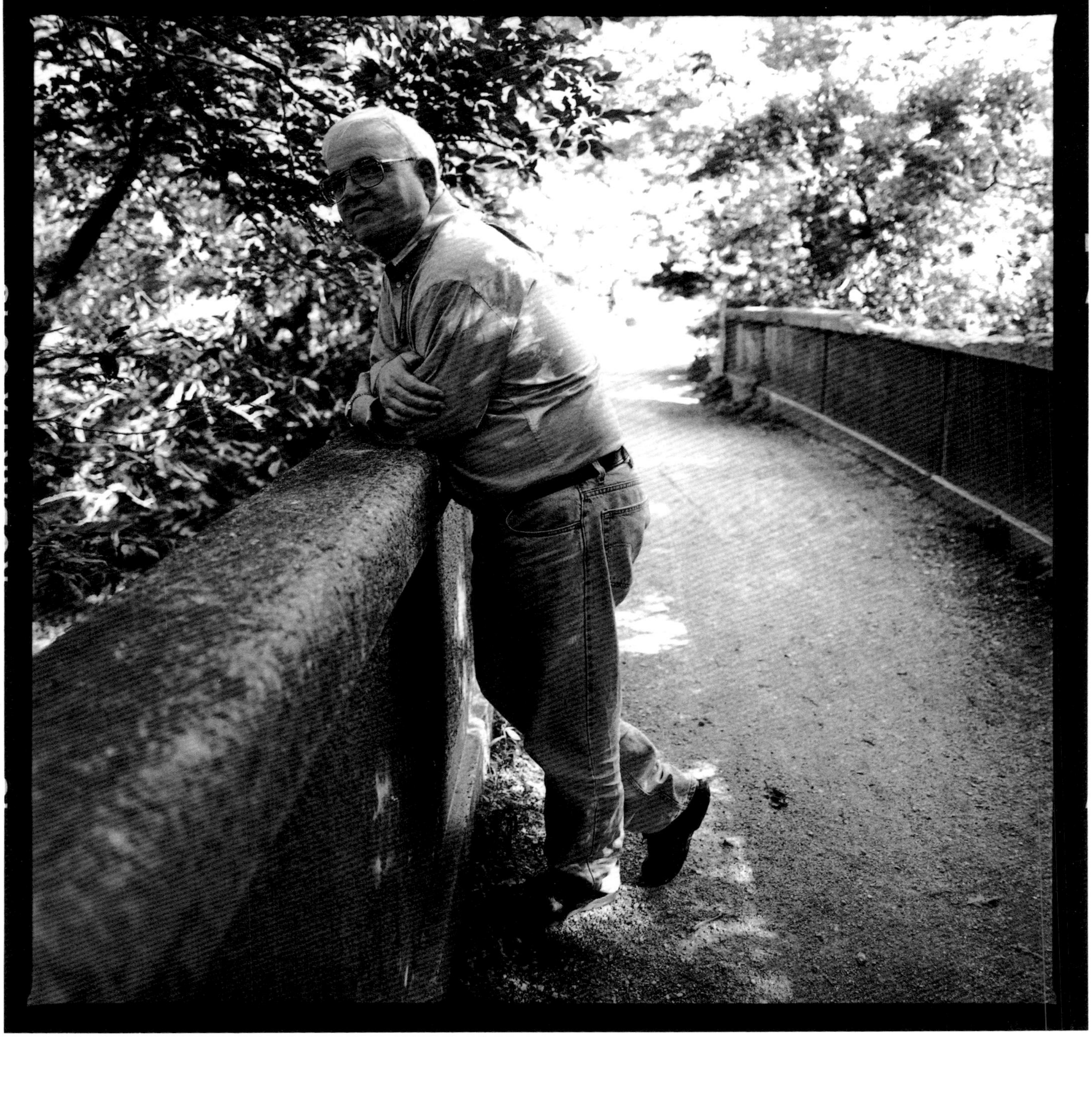

Bruce Goodson

I had a running argument with my therapist Jeff about not feeling well enough to come to the Lockport Center on some days. He said that those are the days we want you to come the most.

Trinity was very good for me as a transition from the hospital and back into the work place. Jeff did a few things that stick out in my mind. I remember having a lot of anger when I started coming to day treatment. He wanted me to talk to him if I felt angry. We also had a comparison thing going on about the forest, which was supposed to represent my progress with my bipolar disorder. He's say to me, "So, how far along are you in the forest today?" And whenever I missed a day at the center he would say, "Now, that'll be enough. I want you to attend therapy sessions and stay out of the smokers' lounge."

Bruce works full-time testing electronic boards for the telephone industry, and has recently celebrated two years of working at a local company. After a breakdown in 1995, he was relieved from his job and spent many hours talking with personnel representatives about getting his job back. His psychiatrist wrote a letter explaining that Bruce was out of work on a legitimate medical excuse and was now able to work again.

Working is what I needed for therapy at that point in my treatment. I was worried about financial problems and paying back the hospital bills.

Today, Bruce is an outpatient, and meets with Jeff regularly for follow-up therapy. He's working, paying back hospital bills, and recently contributed to the down payment for a home.

For me, I have to take the medication for my manic depression and day by day work on my confidence. It's kind of nice when I return to the center for therapy, because I see a lot of the different people who worked with me along the way.

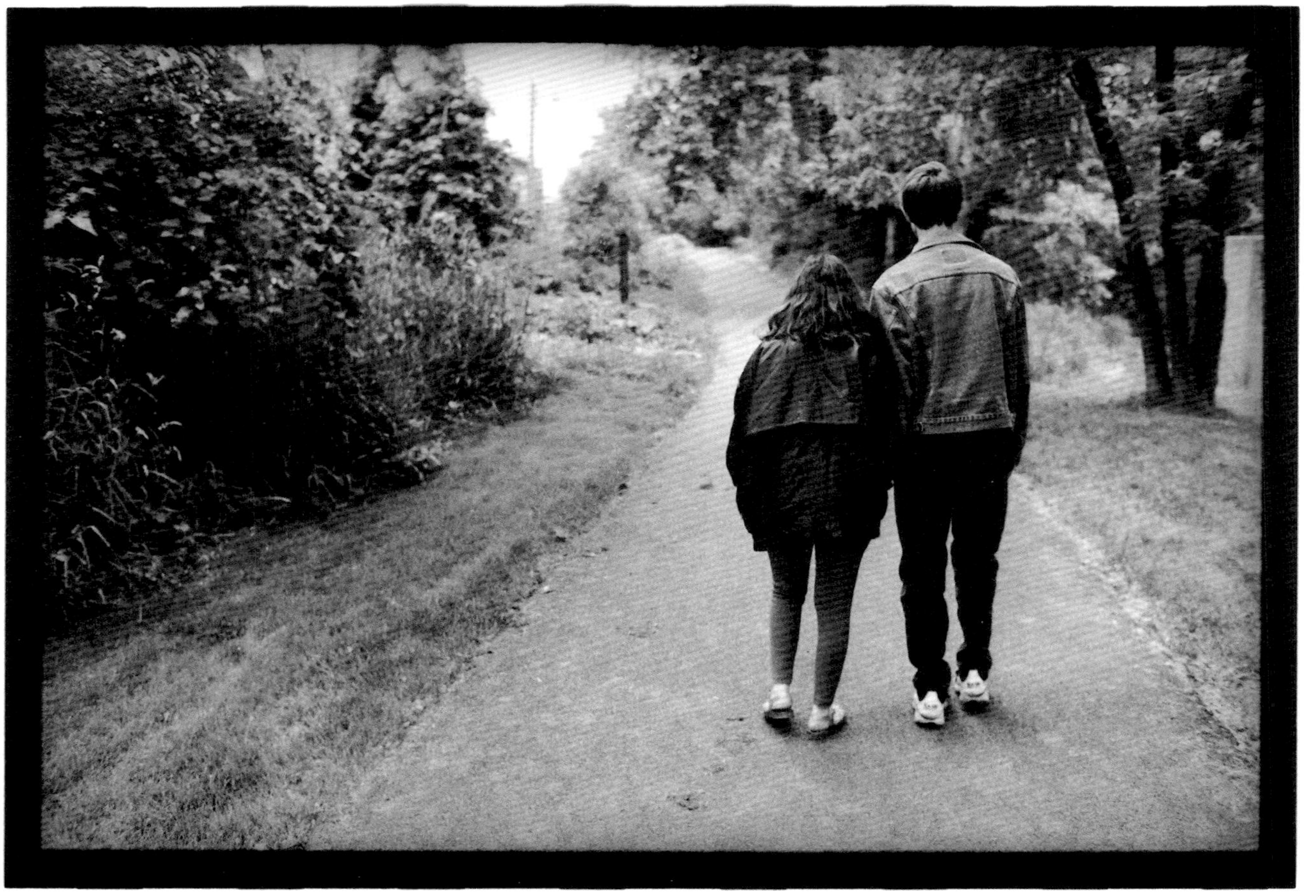

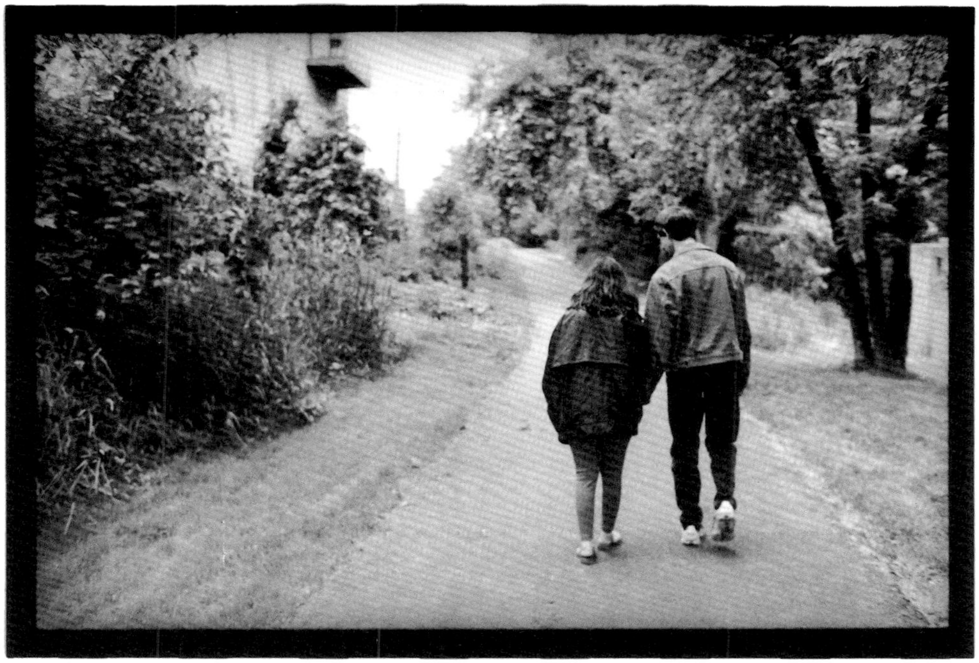

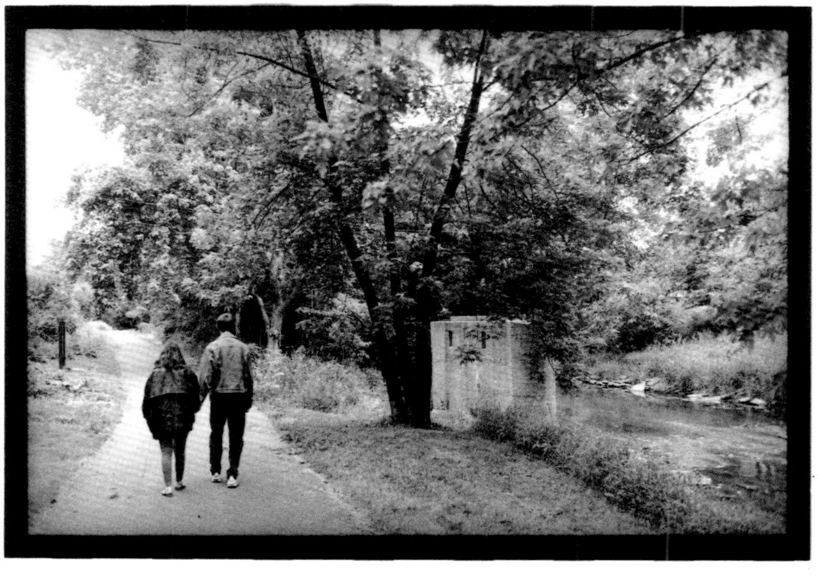

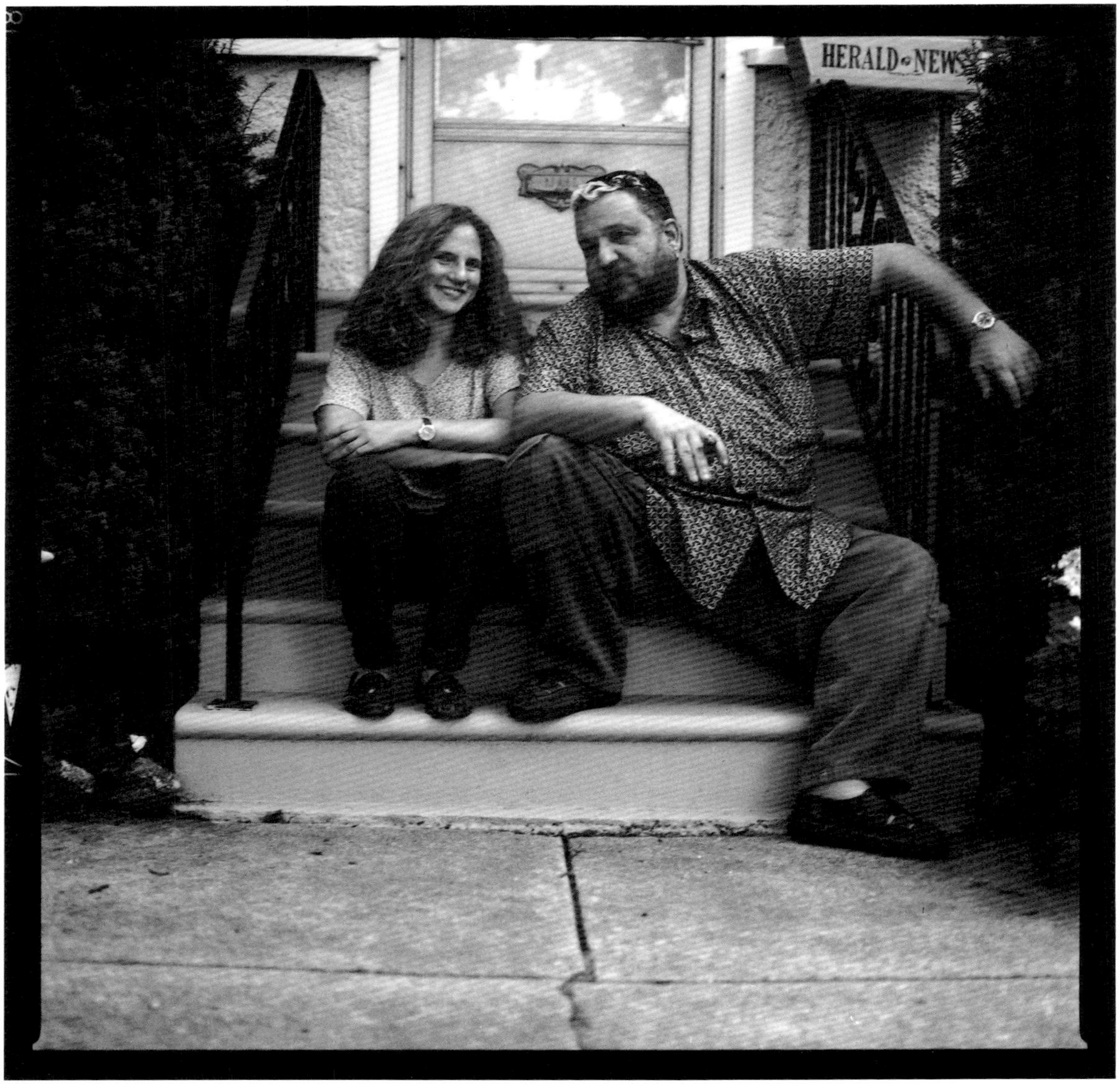

Britt Fohrman

About the Authors

Marc Hauser has been a professional portrait photographer for thirty years. He started by gaining an apprentice position with renowned fashion photographer Stan Malinowski at age fourteen. As a teenager he produced hundreds of album covers with Album Graphics for such artists as The Rolling Stones, Joe Cocker, The Eagles, Jerry Lee Lewis, Rod Stewart, and Jim Morrison. He has won more than a hundred awards for his photography, including a Platinum record for his John Mellencamp album cover, and numerous awards for the well-known "Perception and Reality" ad campaign for *Rolling Stone* magazine. He is best known for his revealing portraits of such celebrities as Michael Jordan, Mar el Hemingway, Aaron Copland, Woody Allen, Sophia Loren, Jim Belushi, Mike Ditka, and Dennis Rodman — the billboard made from Rodman's portrait stopped traffic on Chicago's Kennedy Expressway.

Marc has published three books — *Portraits of Friends and Acquaintances*, *Halloween in Bucktown*, and *Road Pirates*. He is a sought-after speaker who has lectured for Hasselblad, Ilford, Fuji, Mamiya, Polaroid, and Kodak. He lives in Chicago, Illinois.

Alisa Hauser is a social rehabilitation counselor, freelance writer, and former newspaper reporter. She lives in Lockport, Illinois.

Marc and Alisa are second cousins, once removed, who did not meet until they collaborated on this book.

A Note on the Type

The text of this book was set in Frutiger, a typeface originally intended as part of a signage system suited to the architecture of the new Charles de Gaulle Airport outside Paris in 1968. Adrian Frutiger designed this highly legible, simple, robust sans serif type for the airport signage and then completed the typeface family for the Stempel foundry in 1976. Unlike many other sans serif typefaces, which evoke a hardness and sterility, Frutiger possesses a warmth and accessibility that makes for excellent readability. It has a universal quality that makes it appropriate for many applications. The text of this book was set electronically.

Printed and bound by C&C Offset Printing Co., Ltd.
Hong Kong

Designed by Alex Lubertozzi